आमची *Aamchi*

MUMBAI
NAVI MUMBAI & THANE
Tourist Guide Map

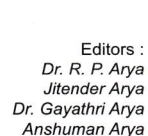

Editors :
Dr. R. P. Arya
Jitender Arya
Dr. Gayathri Arya
Anshuman Arya

IMS

INDIAN MAP SERVICE इण्डियन मैप सर्विस

"Pushkar Estate", Near Ram Mandir, Sector 'G', Shastri Nagar, Jodhpur - 342 003 (Rajasthan) INDIA
Tel. : + 91 291 2612871, 2612872, 2612873, 2740574   Fax : + 91 291 2612870
Website : indianmapservice.co.in   E-mail: indianmapservice@yahoo.co.in

Contents

Introduction	3
Historical Landmarks	6
Touch Mumbai	8
Historical & Heritage Sites	12
Museums & Memorials	21
Beaches, Parks & Garden	27
Other Places	31
Sacred Sites	36
Around Mumbai	42
Festivals	47
Shopping	50
Accommodation & Restaurants	55
Thane Map	60
Nariman Point / Colaba Map	62
Horniman Circle Map	64

Introduction

Introduction

Welcome to...
आमची Aamchi
MUMBAI

GENERAL INFORMATION

Location	: 18.54°N ; 72.4°E	**Rainfall**	: Avg. 216 cm (Jun.-Sept.)
Area	: 600 sq. kms.	**Temperatures:**	
Population	: 12478447	Winter	: 30° C to 19° C
Altitude	: Sea Level	Summer	: 34° C to 27° C
Languages	: Marathi, English, Hindi, Gujarati	**Best Season:**	October to April
		Clothing	: Tropical Cottons
Climate	: Warm Tropical		

Marvellous Mumbai, the capital city of Maharashtra is often referred as the 'Economic Power House of India'. The financial and commercial capital of India is a modern metropolis as well as a living museum of the British era in India. It was originally a cluster of seven islands namely, Colaba, Fort, Byculla, Parel, Worli, Matunga and Mahim, which have been linked through successive reclamations. The earliest inhabitants of these low-lying swampy mud-flats were the Koli fisher-folk and the metropolis derives its name from Mumbadevi, the patron goddess of the Koli's. In 1534, the seven islands were ceded to Portugal by the Sultan of Gujarat in the 'Treaty of Bassein'. The major island of the group Mumbadevi was passed on to Britishers in 1661 as part of the dowry when Catherine of Braganza married England's Charles II.

In 1665, the British occupied all the seven islands and leased them to East India

Introduction

Company. Mumbai witnessed a steady progress under the British. By 1708, it had become the trading headquarters of the western coast of India. The 1800's saw the turning point in the development of Mumbai. The major landmarks were - India's first train journey steaming off from Mumbai to Thane in 1853 ; A major land reclamation project in 1862, joining the original seven islands and later on dismantling of old fort walls by Governor Sir Bartle Frere and initiating a major building boom. Since independence, Mumbai has achieved mind boggling growth. Even the natives of the town find difficult to keep pace with its development activities.

Today, the vibrant metropolis presents a true cosmopolitan outlook, spearheading India's move into the new millennium. It has been transformed from muddy swamps to one of the most important business and industrial centres of the East. It has country's busiest international airport and one of the busiest sea ports of the world, which handles nearly 50% of India's total foreign trade. Mumbai, the nation's industrial heartland, has always been the first choice and a stronghold of the private entrepreneur. An important manufacturing centre for everything, ranging from cars and bicycles to pharmaceuticals and petrochemicals. It has been the most important base for all the multinational companies arriving into the country as a result of economic liberalisation.

Mumbai reflects unusual diversity in all its forms - It is not only the city of commercial and financial activities, but is also the city of temples, churches, mosques, synagogues and host of minor shrines; it is the city of tall sky scrapers as well as wide sprawling slums, one of them being the biggest in Asia ; it is the city of age old traditions and high fashions, the industrialists haven and the largest movie making centre of the world.

Mumbai, the largest city of India is not only the gateway to Maharashtra but is traditionally considered the 'Gateway to India'. This bustling city that never sleeps offers a visitor a multitude of dazzling attractions - wonderful shopping arcades and malls, entertainment- modern and classical, night clubs and discotheques, a wide variety of superb cuisine, splendid museums and art galleries, interesting sight seeings and much more.

Today, the history of Mumbai is a true tribute to the enterprise and vision of its citizens.

Historical Landmarks

3rd BC	–	The islands were under the Mauryan Empire.
2nd BC – 9th AD	–	The islands were under the reign of various dynasties like Satavahanas, Abhiras, Vakatakas, Kalchuris, Konkan Mauryas, Chalukyas and Rashtrakutas.
810-1260 AD	–	Mumbai islands were under the reigns of the Silhara Kings.
1348	–	The islands were captured by Muslim rulers of Gujarat.
1391 – 1534	–	Islands were under the governance of Gujarat Sultanate.
1526	–	Portuguese established factory at Bassein.
1534	–	"Treaty of Bassein" signed between Portuguese viceroy Nuno da Cunha and Bahadur Shah of Gujarat Sultanate, which brought the islands under the possession of the Portuguese.
1554	–	The islands of Mumbai were given to Dr. Garcia da Orta, a Portuguese Physician and Botanist on a yearly rent of £ 85.
1640	–	The first Parsi, Dorabji Nanabhoy Patel arrived in Bombay.
1661	–	The main island of Bombay was presented as dowry to King Charles II of England, when he married Princess Catherine de Braganza of Portugal.
1668	–	King Charles II leased island of Bombay for £10 a year to British East India Co.
1715	–	Fortification built around the commercial and administrative buildings and residential areas by the British Governor Boone.
1794	–	Presidency General Post Office established.
1805	–	Sion Causeway completed.
1826	–	Colaba Observatory completed.
1829	–	The Mint completed.
1833	–	Town Hall completed.
1838	–	Colaba Causeway completed.
1843	–	Establishment of Grant Medical College and J. J. Hospital.
1853	–	Central Railway opened and first ever commercial railway journey (between Bombay and Thane) on the sub-continent.
1854	–	Initiation of Textile industry.
1857	–	Establishment of Bombay University.
1860	–	First water supply drawn from Vihar Lake.
1862	–	The 7 islands were joined under the Land Reclamation Scheme.

Historical Landmarks

1865	–	First gas lamp lit in Bombay.
1869	–	Statue of Roman Goddess of Spring installed at Flora Fountain in memory of Sir Bartle Frere.
1872	–	Establishment of Bombay Municipal Corporation.
1873	–	Establishment of Bombay Port Trust.
1874	–	Tramways introduced.
1875	–	Establishment of Stock Exchange.
1878	–	Rajabai Tower built and High Court building completed.
1880	–	Pherozshah Mehta Gardens built.
1881	–	Malabar Reservoir completed.
1882	–	Introduction of electric lights.
1893	–	Completion of Bombay Municipal Corporation building.
1905	–	Telephone Exchange opened.
1907	–	First electric train from Bombay.
1911	–	King George and Queen Mary enter through Gateway of India. Taxi service introduced.
1914	–	Prince of Wales Museum opened.
1920	–	First airport in India.
1926	–	Introduction of BEST buses.
1935	–	Starting of Marine Drive promenade and the Reserve Bank of India.
1942	–	Quit India Movement launched.
1945	–	Greater Bombay came into being.
1952	–	Jehangir Art Gallery built, endowment by Sir Cawasji Jehangir. Kamla Nehru Park built
1957	–	Opening of Bhabha Atomic Research Centre.
1960	–	Bombay State divided into Gujarat and Maharashtra.
1971	–	International airport at Sahar.
1995	–	Bombay renamed as Mumbai after the patron deity Goddess Mumba Devi.

Touch Mumbai

Touch Mumbai

BY AIR : Mumbai is a major international airport of the country. Many international airlines operate flights to Mumbai from various parts of the world. Indian Airlines and many private airlines cater to the domestic circuit and connect Mumbai to major cities of the country. The two airports Sahar (international) and Santacruz (domestic) are located adjacent to each other. Regular coaches are available between international and domestic airport, which take about 20 minutes time.

AIRLINES DOMESTIC

Air India	1800227722	IA Call Centre (24 Hrs.)	1407
Air India	22876363	IA Toll Free	18001801407
Air India Airport	26118392	Tele-Check in	26156651
Air India Reservation	1406	Jet Airways	39893333
Air India Flight Enq.	1410, 1411	Deccan / Kingfisher	18001800101
Baggage	28318110	Spicejet	18001803333
AI Airport	26168000	Indigo	18001803838
AI Booking Office	22023131	Go Air	1800222111

BY RAIL : Mumbai is one of the important railway centres of the country. It is also the headquarters of the Central and Western Railways. Regular trains connect it with all major cities. There are six major railway stations in the city : Chhatrapati Shivaji Terminus (CST), Mumbai Central, Dadar, Churchgate, Lokmanya Tilak (T) (Kurla) & Bandra T.

RAILWAY ENQUIRY

Railway Enquiry for all information 139
Emergency (Accident / Injury / Death) 22620800
For P.N.R. : Dial 139 + 10 Digit P.N.R. No.
Train **Arrival / Departure** : Dial 139 + 5 Digit Train No.
Just SMS : Simply type **TRAIN** & sent it to **676747**
Websites : http://www.wr.railnet.gov.in (For online train)

BY ROAD : Well connected by good motorable roads with other tourist centres of the region. It is an important junction on the National Highway network of the country. National Highways No. 3, 4, 6, 8, 9 and 17 radiate from the city providing links to all parts of the country. The recently inaugurated express way connecting Mumbai and Pune is a landmark in Indian Roadways history.

BUS SERVICE : Maharashtra State Transport (M.S.R.T.C.) and other transport companies operate regular bus services in the region. The main bus terminus is at - Mumbai Central, S. T. Depot.

MAHARASHTRA STATE TRANSPORT TEL. No.'s.

Mumbai Central	23074272	Sion	24074157
Parel	24211410	Borivali	28931226
Kurla-Nehru Nagar	25222072	Chembur, Maitri Park	25209902
Dadar-Pune Asiad	24136835	Nasik Shirdi	24302667

Local Transport

Mumbai has well developed internal transport system, which includes local trains, buses, taxis, auto-rickshaws, and hovercraft services.

TRAINS : Mumbai sub-urban rail network, is the most over worked and over crowded transport system in the world, but is also one of the best mode to commute in the city. It operates between 0430 hrs. to 0130 hrs. on three lines - Western, Central and Harbour. The Central line operates 1,082 trains carrying about 3.4 million commuters per day and the Western line has 961 trains carrying about 3 million commuters every day. The trains are fast, economical and punctual.

MONORAIL : The Mumbai Monorail is under construction and will be the first monorail system in India. The construction of this ambitious project began in November 2008. Once fully completed it will be the second longest monorail project in the world. The first section of the monorail project was tested successfully between Wadala depot to Mysore colony, covering a distance of approximately 4 kilometers. The section between Wadala and Chembur is believed to be operational by mid 2012.

The proposed monorail routes in the Phase 1 expected to be complete by 2015 are-

- Chembur-Wadala-Jacob Circle (Ghadge Maharaj Chowk)–19.54 kms.
- Mulund – Goregaon – Borivali – 30 kms.
- Virar – Chikhaldongri – 4.60 kms.
- Lokhandwala – SEEPZ – Kanjurmarg – 13.14 kms.
- Thane – Mira – Bhayandar – Dahisar – 24.5 kms.

BUSES : BEST & Co. provides bus services in most parts the city. There are Limited, Ordinary and Air-conditioned buses. The double decker buses are best for short distance travel.

TAXIS : Metered yellow top taxis are available all over the city. Silver and blue coloured air conditioned and mobile despatched taxis called as 'Cool Cabs' have also been introduced here.

AUTO RICKSHAWS : The auto rickshaws are available only beyond Sion on Central line and Bandra on Western line.

HOVERCRAFT SERVICES : This service is available between Gateway of India and New Mumbai.

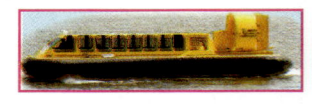

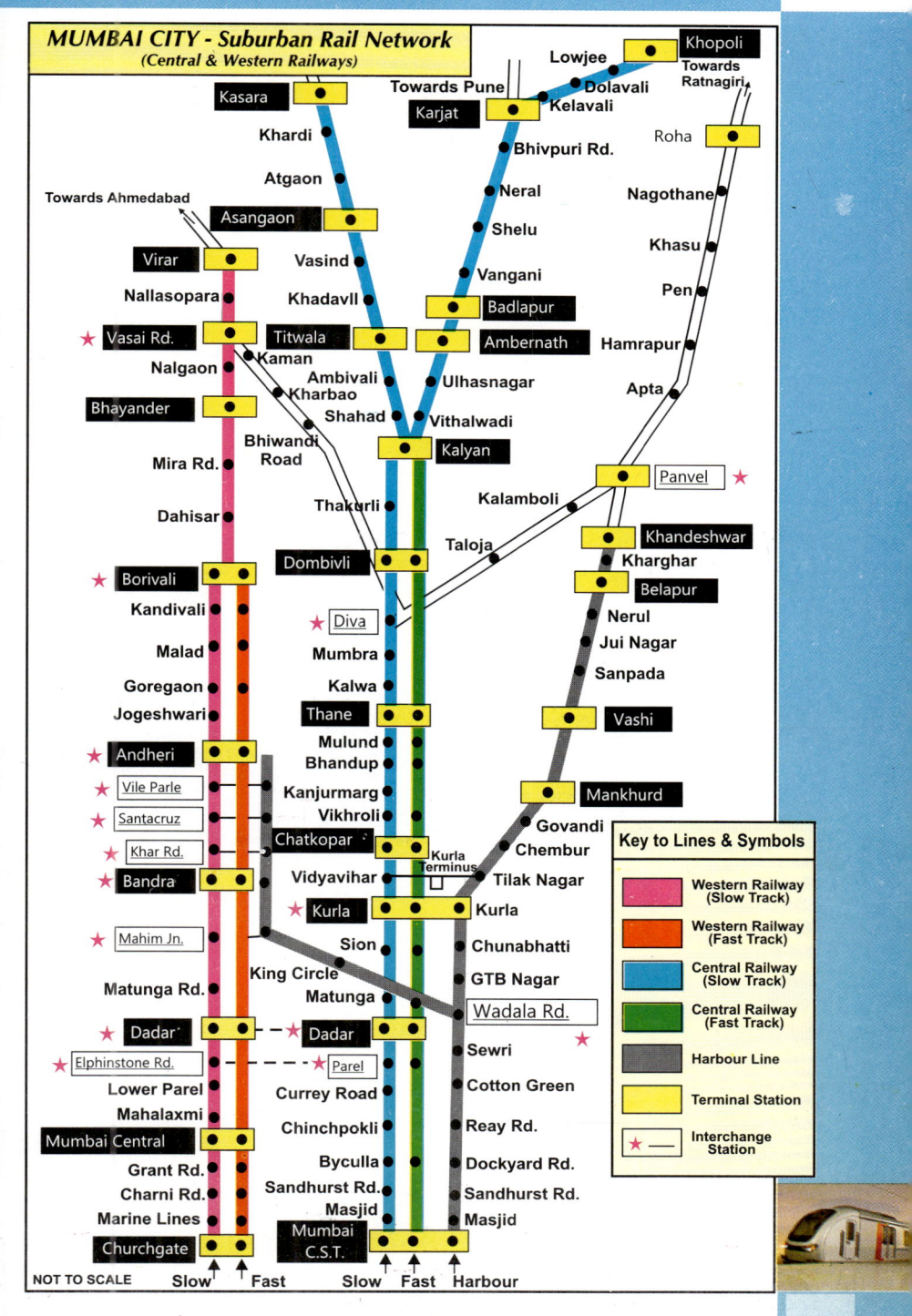

Suburban Rail Network

MUMBAI CITY - Suburban Rail Network
(Central & Western Railways)

Central Railway (Slow/Fast) – Kasara/Khopoli lines:
Towards Pune, Towards Ratnagiri
Khopoli, Lowjee, Dolavali, Kelavali, Karjat, Bhivpuri Rd., Neral, Shelu, Vangani, Badlapur, Ambernath, Ulhasnagar, Vithalwadi, Kalyan
Kasara, Khardi, Atgaon, Asangaon, Vasind, Khadavli, Titwala, Kaman, Ambivali, Kharbao, Shahad
Bhiwandi Road, Thakurli, Dombivli, Diva, Mumbra, Kalwa, Thane, Mulund, Bhandup, Kanjurmarg, Vikhroli, Chatkopar, Vidyavihar, Kurla, Sion, King Circle, Matunga, Dadar, Parel, Currey Road, Chinchpokli, Byculla, Sandhurst Rd., Masjid, Mumbai C.S.T.

Harbour Line:
Panvel, Khandeshwar, Kharghar, Belapur, Nerul, Jui Nagar, Sanpada, Vashi, Mankhurd, Govandi, Chembur, Tilak Nagar, Kurla Terminus, Kurla, Chunabhatti, GTB Nagar, Wadala Rd., Sewri, Cotton Green, Reay Rd., Dockyard Rd., Sandhurst Rd., Masjid

Towards Ratnagiri: Roha, Nagothane, Khasu, Pen, Hamrapur, Apta

Western Railway (Slow/Fast):
Towards Ahmedabad
Virar, Nallasopara, Vasai Rd., Nalgaon, Bhayander, Mira Rd., Dahisar, Borivali, Kandivali, Malad, Goregaon, Jogeshwari, Andheri, Vile Parle, Santacruz, Khar Rd., Bandra, Mahim Jn., Matunga Rd., Dadar, Elphinstone Rd., Lower Parel, Mahalaxmi, Mumbai Central, Grant Rd., Charni Rd., Marine Lines, Churchgate

NOT TO SCALE — Slow, Fast, Slow, Fast, Harbour

Key to Lines & Symbols
- Western Railway (Slow Track) — pink
- Western Railway (Fast Track) — orange
- Central Railway (Slow Track) — blue
- Central Railway (Fast Track) — green
- Harbour Line — grey
- Terminal Station — yellow
- ★ — Interchange Station

Historical & Heritage Sites

Historical & Heritage Sites

Gateway of India

Gateway of India

The 26 metres high archway is the prominent landmark of Mumbai. Originally, it was an iron shed, with carved roofs and served as a makeshift shelter for sea weary passengers in early British period. The structure was replaced by a temporary pavilion and hall in white plaster to welcome King George V and Queen Mary to India in 1911. Lord Sydenham, the then Governor, initiated the plan to build a more permanent structure at the site to commemorate the visit of king. The colossal stone structure was designed by George Wittet. The foundation stone of the present structure was laid in 1913 and the archway was completed in 1927. Ironically, the Gateway was never used for any triumphal receptions for British royalty, but was a mute sentinel to dawn of Indian independence as the last of British troops in India left from here.

The gateway is made of attractive, honey-coloured yellow basalt, obtained near Mumbai, but the stone used for pierced stonework was brought from Gwalior in Madhya Pradesh. The architecture is a magnificent blend between the Paris Arc d'Triomphe, a domed and minareted Moorish palace and Muslim style of 16th century old Gujarat mansion. The gateway has a main large arch, flanked by two smaller arches, at the top are four spires enclosing a small space with balconies on either side. The perforated and attractively fretted stone work above the arches are inspired from the decorative stone work of 16th century Gujarat. Near the main arch is a staircase, tucked away behind small black doors, which previously took the visitors to a breezy balcony enclosed by four spires. An equestrian statue of Chhatrapati Shivaji and statue of Swami Vivekananda have been installed here. There are plenty of launches and cruisers anchored in the sea near the archway, which carry tourists to the famous Elephanta Caves.

Historical & Heritage Sites

Hotel Taj Mahal

Taj Mahal Hotel

The world famous hotel in front of Gateway of India is a very well known site of Mumbai. Jamshetji Nusserwanji Tata, the famous Parsi industrialist built this magnificent hotel in 1899 and was first opened for visitors on 16 Dec. 1903. Some believe that when Jamshetji was refused entry to Watson's hotel on Esplanade, as he was 'a native', he vowed to make a hotel of his own, which would outshine the Watson's. This excellent piece of architecture was designed by W. Chambers, of a local firm of architects and was constructed contrary to the popular myth, the right way round. Jamshetji equipped the Taj with its own electric laundry, Turkish baths, post office, chemist shop and resident doctor. The original red domed structure has been adjoined by a modern skyscraper called as the Taj Mahal Inter-Continental. The Sea Lounge of the hotel affords a fine view of the city.

The streets behind the hotel at Colaba Causeway renamed as Shahid Bhagat Singh Marg are travellers centre of Mumbai. It is a hub of cheap and good hotels and restaurants and a shoppers treasure trove.

S.P. Mukherjee Chowk (Wellington Fountain & Circle)

The Wellington Fountain at the busy roundabout near Gateway of India was built in 1865 to commemorate the visit of Duke of Wellington in 1861 and 1864.

Maharashtra State Police Headquarters (Old Council Hall)

The graceful Byzantine styled structure was once used as a Sailor's Home. It was designed by F. W. Stevens and was built on the site of Mendham Point, Bombay's early cemetery. The beautiful exteriors are built in blue basalt and white bands, while the corners are made up of exquisitely carved Porbandar stone, which is the work of Lockwood Kipling, founder and principal of the School of Art in Bombay and father of famous writer Rudyard Kipling. Another attractive feature is the splendid sculpture of 'Neptune' placed in the gable. It was executed by a "Mr. Bolton of Cheltenham". The building was taken over by the Government in 1928 and a Council Chamber for the Bombay Legislature was built at the back. Later, the Maharashtra State Legislature Assembly and Council met here.

Historical & Heritage Sites

Town Hall

Asiatic Society (Town Hall)

The colonnaded building overlooking the Horniman circle (Cotton Green) is the pride of Mumbai. The elegant building built entirely of Porbandar stone was designed by Col. T. Cowper of Bombay Engineers and was opened in 1833. It houses the Asiatic Society Library, which was founded to encourage studies in oriental arts and sciences. The beautiful structure is characterised by Grecian portico and fluted Ionic pillars. The inside maintains the classic touch with two rows of handsome Corinthian columns and a floor of fine teak. The line of Ionic columns along its frontage was originally supposed to be a double line and the full number was directly supplied from England, like much of the building materials of the time. However, the design was modified and a single row of columns was planned, the remaining columns were used for a classic style church in Byculla.

The upper storey of the building houses the library of the Bombay Asiatic Society which was founded in 1804, by Sir James Macintosh for the investigation and encourage-ment of oriental arts and sciences. It has a collection of over 100,000 volumes of choice literature. The grand Assembly Room has magnificent statues of Chantrey of Governor Mountstuart Elphinstone; Governor Sir J. Malcolm of Forbes, the famous Bombay merchant; Woolner's statue of Sir Bartle Frere, Marochetti's statue of Sir Jamshetiji Jeejeebhoy and one of Jaganath Sankershett, the first Indian member of Asiatic Society.

Mumbai Mint

The majestic building near the Town Hall dates back to 1829. It was designed by Major J. Hawkins of Bombay Engineers and is noted for its Ionic portico. The historical landmark was built on the land reclaimed from sea and can now only be seen with prior permission from the Mint Master.

Mumbai University

The university was founded in 1857 and has some of the finest buildings of south Mumbai. The main buildings are the Senate Hall and the University Library with its Rajabai Clock Tower.

The **University Hall** is named after Sir Cowasjee Jehangir, who donated generously for its construction. The hall is built in French decorative style of 15th century from designs sent out from England by George Gilbert Scott, a prolific designer of the times. Its most outstanding features are the delightful, open spiral work staircases. It is 32 m. (104 ft.) long, 13 m. (44 ft.) wide and 19 m. (63 ft.) height to the apex of the groined ceiling, with an apse separated from the hall by a grand arch and a gallery. The profusion of stained glass windows produces interesting effects with light. In front of the hall is the statue of Sir Cowasjee.

The 19th century **University Library** and **Rajabai Clock Tower** are built in Venetian

Rajabai Clock Tower

15

Historical & Heritage Sites

Gothic style and were also designed by George Gilbert Scott.

The 79 metres Rajabai Clock Tower is a part of University library and is one of the finest buildings and most conspicuous landmark of south Mumbai. The octagonal lantern - shaped tower was built by Premchand Raichand, a wealthy merchant, in memory of his mother Rajabai. This excellent piece of architecture is crowned by a spire with twenty carved figures in the niches representing the different castes of western India. An opening in the centre of each floor contains the great clock which once pealed forth hymns on Sundays and favourites like 'God Save the King' on weekdays. Below the dials on the outer side are four small galleries with balustrades. The clock tower from here commands a fine view of the city, with the Harbour and Mody Bay to the east and Malabar Hill and Backbay to the west.

High Court

The imposing white-pinnacled and blue basalt building was built in 1878. It was designed by General A. Fuller in English Gothic style. The 169 metres high building with its central structure rising to 54.2 metres was opened in 1879. The entrance is through a large arched porch flanked by two octagonal 36 metres high towers, surmounted by statues representing Justice and Mercy.

The interiors are decorated with dark, polished teak ceiling with an elaborately carved centrepiece and floor of Italian mosaic. The pillared galleries are ornately carved with humorous and satirical carvings depicting themes like, apes at play, a half-blind ape holding the scales of justice, a fox wearing a barrister's bands, a pig and a tiger in a fight, birds swooping in and out of carved stones shrubbery etc. Most of these carvings were done by Indian stone masons.

Flora Fountain (Hutatma Chowk)

The stone figure of Flora, the Roman Goddess of Flowers - Flora, stands at the junction of five busy streets. The statue is surrounded by fountains and host of mythological figures. It was built in honour of Sir Bartle Frere, Governor of Bombay (1862 - 1867), who is known for his town planning of Bombay and many of its Gothic structures. It was designed

Historical & Heritage Sites

Flora Fountain & Martyr's Square

by a committee including R. Norman Shaw. There is also a martyr's memorial in the same premises. Today, the area around the square is a flourishing business centre of Mumbai.

Kala Ghoda

The Kala Ghoda or Black Horse precinct, named after a black stone statue of King Edward VII (earlier Prince of Wales) astride a horse, which was erected at the centre of a node on Mahatma Gandhi Road (Esplanade Rd.) is bounded by the Fountain district in the north and S.P. Mukherjee Chowk in the south. The statue was built by Albert Abdullah David Sassoon, a Jewish businessman and philanthropist, but was removed in 1965 and sent to the Bhau Daji Lad Museum and now shifted to the Jijamata Udyan in Byculla.

The precinct considered to be a premier art district and cultural hub of the city, holds a unique place in the world of art and culture. It is dotted with important art galleries, outdoor pavement galleries, museums, exhibition spaces, institutions, boutiques, restaurants and grand colonial structures. The area attracts a large number of tourists,

Kala Ghoda Festival

artists, fashion designers, architecture enthusiasts and food lovers from all corners of the world, especially during the annual Kala Ghoda Arts Festival. It also buzzes with cultural activities held by educational and art institutions and the Crafts Festival organised by the State Government.

The nine day Kala Ghoda Arts Festival organised by Kala Ghoda Association in late January or early February, started in 1999 and has now emerged as one of the most popular events of this truly cosmopolitan metropolis.

One can enjoy delicacies at different food stalls and see master craftsmen at work and buy their wares at the Kala Ghoda festival. Talented painters make sketches and portraits and sell them at reasonable price.

Historical & Heritage Sites

Chhatrapati Shivaji Terminus

Brihan Mumbai Mahanagar Palika

Chhatrapati Shivaji Terminus

The majestic railway station was earlier called as the Victoria Terminus (V.T) and is the first railway terminus of the country. It is also one of the largest and oldest train terminuses of the east. The modern terminus is also regarded as one of the most magnificent railway stations of the world. The imposing structure in Gothic style, was designed by J.W. Stevens and is one of the most spectacular buildings of the city. It was built over a period of ten year from 1878 - 88 at a cost of Rs. 16,35,562/-. The building is an exotic blend of Italian medieval Gothic and the opulent Mughal mausoleum architectural styles. It is adorned with turrets and elegant columns of fine Italian marble and polished Indian blue stone. The archways are covered with ornately carved foliage, over which are peer gargoyles and other grotesque figures, while well sculpted peacocks flaunt their beauty under the eaves. The ornamental iron work, beautiful stained glass and impressive groined roof in blue and gold decoration add to the beauty of the structure. But, the most impressive is the imposing octagonal shaped dome surmounted by a figure symbolising 'Progress'. The central facade has a large clock measuring 3.19 metres in diameter. The name of the majestic terminus was officially changed to Chhatrapati Shivaji Terminus in 1994. It was also accorded the status of World Hertage Site in 2004, for its considerable heritage and architectural value.

Brihan Mumbai Mahanagar Palika (Municipal Corp. Bldg.)

The magnificent building stands opposite to Chhatrapati Shivaji Terminus. It was designed by F. W. Stevens in early Gothic style, blended with Indian motifs. The building was opened in 1893 and has an impressive 78 metres high tower, crowned with a spectacular dome. The octagonal minarets flank the corners and the building has typical Gothic arched windows. Over the central gable on the south side stands a 4 metre allegorical

Historical & Heritage Sites

Elphinstone College

statue representing the title Bombay proudly adopted - Urbs primus in Indis (meaning the first city of India), with the arms of the Municipal Corporation contained in a circular panel beneath it. In front of the building is a statue of Sir Pherozeshah Mehta, known for his contribution towards the civic life of early Bombay.

Headquarters of Western Railway

The architectural masterpiece located adjacent to the Church Gate railway station houses the Headquarters of the Western Railways. It was completed in 1897 and is decorated by a sculpted group depicting engineering, commerce and agriculture.

Elphinstone College

The college was shifted from its first premises in Byculla to this large Romanesque style building in 1890. It was the first institution in India to offer university education. The main hall is named after Sir Cowasjee Jehangir in recognition of his generous contribution

Headquarters of Western Railway

to the original institution founded as a memorial to Gov. Mountstuart Elphinstone in 1856.

Hafkine's Institute (Govt. House), Parel

In 1673, the Jesuits built a church and convent on the site of the ancient temple of Pareli Vaijnath, from which the area took its name. In 1719, Governor Boone took over the convent and used it as a country house. The first governor to make it his official residence was William Hornby between 1771 and 1780. In 1885, Lady Fergusson, wife of the then governor, died of cholera and the place remained vacant until 1897. It was then

19

Historical & Heritage Sites

used as a plague hospital for two years before W. M. Haffkine established his pioneering plague research laboratory here. Today, it houses the famous Haffkine Institute, the country's finest laboratory for bacteriological research. The institute is engaged in the study of tropical medicine and preparation of rabies and plague vaccines.

Dabbawala's - The Illiterate Business Gurus

Dabbawala, the tiffin box carrier or lunchpail - man are one of the unique phenomenons of Mumbai. They bring fresh warm lunch for the office-goers from their homes in far away suburbs of the city, packed in "dabbas" - the cylindrical aluminium cannisters and also collect them after the lunch and return them to their respective homes in time. The lunch delivery tradition was started by Mahadeo Havaji Bachche, about 125 years ago with about 100 men and has now grown to a strength of over 5,000 mostly illiterate deliverymen, handling around 200,000 identical "dabbas" with barely one error in every six million deliveries, for which they have earned a 'Six Sigma Rating', from the prestigious Forbes magazine. It is amazing to note that tiffin delivery system continues efficiently even during the rainy season, when on certain days the city comes to a grinding halt. The dabbawalas operate in a chain and are very well aware that if this chain is broken at any point, thousand of people working in offices will have to go without lunch. The "dabbas" placed in wooden carte bear codes and colour markings, as many deliverymen are illiterate. They are then arranged as per their delivery areas and mostly transported in the local trains. Most of the Dabbawalas get down at Churchgate station, as many offices are located nearby and the tiffins are delivered at right place in right time. The efficient dabbawalas in their Gandhi topis can be seen running headlong into traffic, shouting 'Lafka! Lafka!... meaning Hurry Up!, Hurry Up!... Their amazing working and punctuality has even attracted a large number of celebrities from around the world, right from the charming Prince Charles to Richard Branson. The humble Dabbawalas now also give management lectures at the top business schools and are also developing software that will allow users to book dabba lunch delivery online. One can even email at info@mydabbawala.com to sign up for service. Recently their services have also included cooking of food for delivery.

The dabbawalas have formed the 'Nutan Mumbai Tiffin Box Suppliers Trust', which looks into their welfare and day-to-day problems.

Museums & Memorials

Museums & Memorials

Chhatrapati Shivaji Maharaj Vastu Sangrahalaya

Chhatrapati Shivaji Maharaj Vastu Sangrahalaya (Prince of Wales Museum of Western India)

One of the best museums in the country was originally named after King George V, who as Prince of Wales laid its foundation stone in 1905. The museum is housed in a Moorish style building decorated with blue and yellow basalt work and is surrounded by beautiful garden. There are three main sections — Art, Archaeology and Natural History, which are known for fine collection of miniature paintings, masterpieces of Indian sculpture and Tibetan art. Sections on Forestry and Geology have also been added to the museum. The Maritime Heritage Gallery with articles related to navigation is first of its kind in the country.

The Art section has paintings from the Dutch, British, French and Italian schools, which were mainly given by Sir Ratan Tata. There are also masterpieces like, Cuyp, Lawrence, Romney, Gainsborough, Troyon, Poussin and Titian. One can also see works from the late Italian schools, modern French and British. Indian paintings of Mughal and Rajput schools, as well as an interesting collection of relics of the Satara Rajas are also exhibited. Other attractions of the section are, oriental arms, breathtaking exhibits of jade, fine china, Indian brass, silver and Indian and Persian carpets.

The Archaeological section is divided into three parts — Brahmanical section, section on Jain, pre-historic and foreign antiques and a Buddhist section. The Brahmanical section has large 5th and 6th century bas reliefs, a bust of Lord Siva from the Elephanta Caves, magnificent sculptures of Siva, Brahma and Vishnu and an interesting collection of articles used in Brahmanical worship.

The pre-historic section has palaeolithic and neolithic implements and necropolitan pottery used for coffins, all discovered in the Madras (Chennai) region. Jain sculptures and Mesoptamian bas-reliefs can also be seen here. In the Buddhist section are terracotta figures of Buddha and Bodhisattavas, images and bas-reliefs of the Gandhara school narrating tales from the Jatakas (collection of Buddhist mythologies) and portions of Amaravati's splendid Stupa.

Museums & Memorials

Port Trust War Memorial

Bombay Natural History Society

Bombay Natural History Society

It is located near Prince of Wales museum and is a treasure house of natures wonders. A full floor is devoted to beetles and butterflies arranged taxonomically. Another floor has embalmed reptiles, birds and animal pelts. There is also an extensive library of nature books.

RBI Monetary Museum

The impressive museum housed in the Amar Building at Phiroze Shah Mehta Road in the Fort area, provides an insight into the interesting history of Indian money, dating back to various ancient Indian dynasties, foreign invaders, colonial era to the present time. Coins were prevalent in India since 6th century B.C. and very few countries of the world can match the sheer diversity of coins found here. The museum has a rich and varied collection of coins, notes and currency and is divided into six sections.

Port Trust War Memorial

The memorial at Ballard Estate is set on the junction of Ballard Road, Sprot Road and Narottam Morarji Marg. It was erected in honour of the port officers, who laid down their lives during the World War I and contribution made by the Port Trust in the British war effort. The memorial has a single fluted stone column surmounted by a lantern.

A brass plaque here reads –

"In the Port of Bombay in the Great War 1914-1918.

1,870,000 troops and personnel embarked and disembarked at the docks.

3,046 transports and 668 hospital ships were dealt with at the docks. The first transport left Bombay on 21 August 1914.

2,073 troop and hospital trains were railed over the Port Trust Railway.

2,228,000 tons of military stores were shipped from the port.

494 Government ships used the Port Trust dry docks."

Manibhavan (Gandhi Memorial)

The house where Mahatma Gandhi often stayed, when he visited the city between

Museums & Memorials

Interior of Victoria & Albert Museum

Interiors of Manibhavan

Bhau Daji Lad Museum (Victoria & Albert Museum)

It is set amidst lush Veermata Jijabai Bhonsle Udyan and has a rich collection of archaeological finds, original maps, photographs, prints and paintings depicting the history of Mumbai. Until 1857, the collection was housed in the Fort barracks, but when Sir G. Birdwood was appointed Curator, he raised subscriptions for this building, which was completed in 1871. The clock tower in front was erected by Sir Albert Sasson, who also presented the statue of the Prince Consort by Noble.

In 2004, Mumbai chapter of INTACH (Indian National Trust for Art & Cultural Heritage), financed by the Jamnalal Bajaj Foundation, took up the responsibility of reviving the museum to its old glory. In 2005, it bagged the highest award in conservation - UNESCO's Asia Pacific Heritage Award for Cultural Heritage Conservation. The magnificently refurbished museum celebrated its 150th anniversary in 2007. Over 6,000 exhibits of the museum were also restored painstakingly through years of research and hard work. It has now become one of the must visit sites of the city.

1917 - 1934, has now been converted into a national memorial. It is now one of the important historical landmarks of Mumbai and has been witness to the struggle of freedom movement of India. It was in Mani Bhavan in 1917, that Gandhiji took his first lesson in carding from a carder who passed by every day. He learnt spinning too over here. The 'Satyagraha' against the Rowlatt Act was launched in 1919 from Mani Bhavan. The building now houses a 20,000-volume research library, a film and recording archive and a set of diorama on Gandhiji's life. Of special interest is the room Gandhiji used, which is still intact and unchanged.

Museums & Memorials

Nehru Planetarium

Discovery of India Bldg., Nehru Centre

Nehru Centre

The well known cultural centre at Annie Beasant Road, Worli, next to Mahalaxmi Racecourse was conceived in 1972, commemorating Jawaharlal Nehru's vision of modern, scientific and self reliant India. The 14 storeyed unique cylindrical building of the centre called as 'Discovery of India' is a famous landmark, dominating the skyline of the area and was designed by J. M. Kadri, one of the finest architects of the country. The centre comprises of a fine planetarium, a permanent exhibition named Discovery of India, a Cultural Wing and Art Gallery.

Nehru Planetarium : The large domed building resembling a UFO, houses the planetarium and is the only astronomical centre of the city. It offers a fine lesson in astronomy through sky-shows combining entertainment with instruction. Regular shows unravelling the mysteries of the Universe are held in Hindi, English and Marathi at the planetarium, which are very popular among school kids and other visitors.

Nehru Science Centre : It lies in the Discovery of India building, adjacent to the Nehru Planetarium and is specially designed for children and youth. The children can view and also participate in various scientific activities, which educates and develops scientific aptitude among them. Main highlights of the centre are computer laboratory, mobile science exhibition units, evolution and heritage hall, auditorium, inflatable dome planetarium, science library and children's science park etc.

The centre is also a venue for a number of international trade fairs and local exhibitions.

Discovery of India : The interesting permanent exhibition comprising of 14 galleries is a true introduction of the incredible India. There are over 50,000 exhibits, like replicas of major architectural and artistic works, photographs, models and audio-visuals depicting India's growth in various fields like science, technology, art, society and culture etc.

Museums & Memorials

Nehru Science Museum : The museum showcases the development of science and technology in the country since the beginning of civilization.

Art Gallery : The modern art gallery at the ground floor of the Discovery of India building was established to promote young talent. Works of well known painters and sculptors are also displayed here.

Nehru Auditorium : Various cultural programmes, concerts and plays are held over here.

Also visit the famous 'Jewel of India' restaurant located near Nehru Centre for delectable cuisine.

DR. AMBEDKAR SMARAK, CHAITYABHOOMI, DADAR

Dr. Bhimrao Ambedkar, an eminent political leader and a highly talented multi-faceted personality was the Chairman of the Drafting committee of Indian Constitution. He embraced Buddhism and was cremated at the crematorium near Shivaji Park on 6th December 1956. The site was converted to Chaitya Bhoomi, a National Monument and inaugurated in 1971, by his daughter-in-law, Mrs. Meerabai Yeshvantrao Ambedkar. The square shaped monument with a mezzanine floor is crowned by a small dome. The mezzanine floor has a Stupa and resting place for Buddhist monks. The structure surrounded by a circular wall, rising to a height of about one and a half metres has two entrances, covered with white marble. Within the circular wall are statues of Dr. Ambedkar and Lord Buddha. The monument is beautifully illuminated in the evenings and the tranquil ambience compels you to spend some time here in solitude. A large number of visitors come here from all parts of the country. A special ceremony is held every year on 6th December, when thousands of people gather here to pray and pay homage to Dr. Ambedkar. Buddha Purnima is another important celebration at this sacred site.

Dr. Ambedkar Smarak

Beaches, Parks & Gardens

Beaches, Parks & Gardens

Girgaum Chowpatty Beach

The popular beach at the northern end of Marine Drive has a special place in the life of Mumbaikars. It will not be wrong to term it as the 'Heart of Mumbai' and is the venue for important festivals like Coconut Day and the Ganesh Chaturthi immersions. The beach has been cleaned up recently. Palm and other trees have also been planted

The beach also features in the history of India's freedom struggle, as mass political meetings were held here in the pre-independence era. Statues of great freedom fighters, Lokmanya Tilak and Vithalbhai Patel are erected on the beach.

Erangal Beach

35 kms. by suburban electric train to Malad, thence by road. Hotels and shacks are available at this lovely beach.

Gorai Beach

The clean and calm beach of Gorai is 59 km. from the city centre. Nearest railhead is Borivali, from there by bus or auto to Gorai creek, which has to be crossed by ferry. The famous theme park Essel World is located nearby.

Juhu Beach

The second most popular beach of Mumbai lies on the Bandra-Khar road, about twenty kms. from the city. The crowded beach lined by bungalows and high rise apartments offers various entertainment and amusements.

A number of food stalls here serve local delicacies like, Pav bhaji, bhelpuri, panipuri and various chat and snack items.

Versova Beach

The picturesque beach lies immediately to the north of Juhu beach and the two beaches are separated by a creek.

Madh, Marve & Manori Beaches

These are 44.8 km.,38.4 km. and 40 km. respectively by suburban electric train to Malad, and thence 12 km., 5.6 km. and 6.4 km. respectively by road. Ferry services available from Marve to Manori beach.

Pherozshah Mehta Gardens (Hanging Garden)

The beautiful garden perched atop Malabar Hill, was laid out in 1881, atop a series of water reservoirs which supply water to Mumbai. The well maintained garden has hedges cut in animal and bird shapes. A gigantic clock dial is made entirely out of flower beds. It is also a popular picnic spot and the sun-set view from here is breathtaking.

Beaches, Parks & Gardens

Veermata Jijabai Bhonsle Udhyan

Kamla Nehru Park

Kamla Nehru Park

The children's park is perched on the beautiful slopes of Malabar Hill, just across the road from Hanging Garden. It is named after the wife of Shri Jawahar Lal Nehru, the first prime minister of India. The garden was laid in 1952 and has a variety of delights for children. The "Old Woman's Shoe" along with the swings and slides in the park are very popular. The garden commands a panoramic view of the Marine Drive and Chowpatty Beach.

Veermata Jijabai Bhonsle Udhyan (Victoria Gardens)

The lush garden is a comprehensive complex of a Botanical Garden, Zoo and the famous Dr. Bhau Daji Lad Museum, which has cultural and historical exhibits. The garden was laid out in 1861, on the property donated by David Sassoon, a wealthy Jewish businessman and was named as Victoria Garden and people still call it as Rani Bagh or Queen's Garden.

Mumbai Port Trust Garden

The beautiful garden well maintained by the Mumbai Port Trust, sprawls over an area of 12 acres, near Colaba Causeway and affords a fine view of the Mumbai Port and naval yards. It has been acknowledged as the best garden in the Municipality's Annual Garden Competition on number of occasions. The garden with lush lawns and colourful flowers is equipped with seaside sit-outs, a stone plaza and glass house and is a popular picnic spot. The garden also attracts migratory birds during the winter season.

Lion Safari Park / Krishnagiri Upvan / Sanjay Gandhi N.P.

It is located near Borivalli station, which is 35km. by suburban electric train from the town. The park also called as Krishnagiri Upvan, has the Gandhi Smriti Mandir on Pavilion Hill. The Lion Safari Park provides a great opportunity to view the Indian lion from special, closed vehicles. Kanheri Caves, one of the largest groups of Buddhist caves in western India, are another major attraction of the park.

29

Beaches, Parks & Gardens

Vihar Lake : The scenic lake built in 1860, on the Mithi river now lies within Sanjay Gandhi National Park and is the largest lake of Mumbai. The Tulsi Lake lies to the north and Powai Lake to the south of the Vihar Lake.

Essel World & Water Kingdom

The theme park is about 70 kms. from city centre near Gorai beach and is very popular all over the country. It has lots of exciting rides and games, which are enjoyed by children as well as elders. The entry fee includes unlimited rides. The recently opened Water Kingdom adjacent to the Essel World is a great experience for any water loving individual and is a perfect venue to beat the heat in summers.

Nearest railway station is Malad or Borivalli from where the journey has to be made by road and sea. It is also approachable by road via Bhayandar on Western Express Highway.

Fantasy Land

The amusement park is located at Jogeshwari, about 29 kms. from the city. It is smaller in size and cheaper as compared to Essel World, but is proving to be very popular.
Nearest railway station is Jogeshwari (E).

Other Places

Other Places

Marine Drive

Vidhan Sabha Bhavan, Nariman Point

Taraporewala Aquarium

Netaji Subhash Marg or Marine Drive

It is one of the most beautiful and popular promenades in the world. Reclaimed from the backbay the drive starts from Nariman Point via Chowpatty Beach up to the Malabar Hill. Exhilarating view of the promenade can be enjoyed from Malabar Hill especially at night, when the string of lights on the curve shine like pearls and appear like a 'Queen's Necklace'. It is a favourite haunt for joggers, walkers and breeze lovers.

Nariman Point

This 'piece of Manhattan' transposed to Mumbai is indeed one of the best known commercial addresses, not only of Mumbai but of entire India. The reclaimed land is full of sleek skyscrapers. The area studded with plush offices and restaurants bustles with activity by the day and is almost deserted in the nights.

Taraporewala Aquarium

The aquarium was opened in 1951 and has an exotic collection of marine and fresh water fish. There is also a series of small fish tanks displaying corals, sea flowers, sea horses and other invertebrate forms. An interesting section demonstrates various stages in the growth of a pearl and also displays exquisite pearl and mother-of-pearl jewellery.

Mahalaxmi Dhobi Ghat

The open-air laundry or Dhobi Ghat at the Saat Rasta roundabout, close to the Mahalaxmi railway station is studded with rows of concrete wash pens with flogging stones. One can see around two hundred diligent dhobis (washermen) and their families washing the dirty linen

Other Places

Mahalaxmi Racecourse

by dipping them in soapy water and thrashing on the flogging stones. The place is regarded to be the largest open-air laundry in the world and is a popular site among the foreign tourists.

Mahalaxmi Racecourse

It is one of the finest racecourses of the east. Racing season : Nov. to Apr., on Saturdays and Sundays.

Raj Bhavan (Malabar Hill)

The official residence of the Governor of Maharashtra is set on a promontory amidst lush surroundings. It has been in use since early 1800's and the earliest resident was Governor Evan Nepean (1812 -19). Notable additions to it were a public breakfast room and a detached 'sleeping bungalow' by Elphinstone. The magnificent bungalow affords excellent views of the Mumbai city.

Sir Jamsetjee Jeejeebhoy (J. J.) School of Art

The premier art institute of the country was first started in 1857, but, the present building with sloping tiled roofs and rounded pillars dates back to 1877. Many prominent buildings in western India owe their murals, paintings and decorative railings and carvings to the students of this institution. The ornamental railings and gates of the Victoria Terminus were made at the school.

Weaver's Service Centre

It is located at Pandit Paluskar Chowk (Opera house junction). Preparation of designs, weaving of samples and block printing by hand can be seen with the permission of the Director of the centre.

AAREY Milk Colony

The modern dairy amidst lush gardens is about 35 kms. from city centre and can be approached via Kurla or Andheri, by suburban electric train to Goregaon and thence 3.2km. by road. The Central Dairy is open for visitors from 0900 to 1200 hrs.

Tower of Silence

The Parsi dokhma or burial ground is located at Malabar Hill. Entry to this round stone tower is forbidden except for the attendants of the Tower, who carry the dead body and place them on iron grids inside, where they may not pollute Earth, Water, the Air outside and Fire. Inside the tower, the bodies are consumed by vultures.

Other Places

Worli Dairy
Pasteurising, bottling and distribution of milk can be seen at this massive modern dairy at M. A. Gaffar Khan Rd. Time 0900-1300 hrs & 1400-1600 hrs.

Kabutarkhana, Dadar
Kabutarkhana, the pigeon feeding place near Dadar (W) railway station was built in 1933, by Valamji Ratanshi Vora and is regarded as the 'Trafalgar Square' of the city. The sacred secular spot surrounded by a Jain Temple, a Hanuman Temple, a Mosque and a Cross is quite busy and noisy with heavy vehicular traffic moving around it. It has been acknowledged as a heritage site by the government. People come here to feed the pigeons and the "Dadar Kabootarkhana Trust" also raises funds to feed the birds. Grains like channa, moong, jowar, bajra, corn etc. are provided for the pigeons, who according to an estimate consume over 1,500 kgs. of grain everyday. The Bombay Veterinary College at Parel, looks after the health of the pigeons, multivitamins are dissolved in the water for pigeons to boost their immunity.

DHARAVI

Dharavi, one of the largest slums of the world has been in news for all the wrong reasons, over the years. The narrow alleys of Dharavi not only symbolises poverty, crime and unhygienic living conditions, but also depicts strong human endeavours, determination and will to succeed and survive amidst the most unfavourable conditions. Mumbai city has attracted a large flow of immigrant population searching for work and better living conditions, which has resulted into growth of slums and shanties, where about 55 % of the city's population reside.

The Dharavi slum sprawls over an area of 1.75 sq. kms. and is home to over one million people. Mithi River in the north and Sion and Matunga in the south and east. The Migrants from various states came here with time and initiated their traditional works of pottery, tanneries and embroidery work etc. Today, Dharavi is also a thriving centre of small scale industry of the city with about 5,000 flourishing businesses and 15,000 single room factories engaged in different works like pottery, leather tanning, readymade garments, bakery, plastic goods, soap factory and recycling industry etc.

Tourists interested to explore and experience this facet of Mumbai can also undertake a 'Slum Tour', organized by various agencies like Reality Tours and Travel. They take you around the slum showing the indomitable spirit of the Dharavi residents.

Dharavi Slums

Other Places

BANDRA WORLI SEA LINK

The Bandra Worli Sea Link (BWSL), officially named as the Rajiv Gandhi Sea Link, is a cable-stayed bridge with pre-stressed concrete viaduct approaches, linking Bandra and the western suburbs of Mumbai with Worli and central Mumbai. This marvel of engineering is India's first road bridge across the sea and the latest attraction of Mumbai. It reduces the travel time between Bandra and Worli from 45 - 60 minutes to seven minutes.

Some of the salient features of the sea-link are:

- The prestigious project was implemented by the Maharashtra State Road Dev. Corpn. (MSRDC) and built by HCC (Hindustan Construction Company) at a cost of about Rs. 1634 crores.
- Experts from various countries like Canada, China, Egypt, Hong Kong, Indonesia, Philippines, Serbia, Singapore, Switzerland and United Kingdom assisted the Indian engineers.
- The length of the entire project is 5.6 kms., connecting Express Highway and Swami Vivekanand road at Bandra to Worli at Worli end. The length of the bridge (4.7 kms.) is 63 times the height of the Qutub Minar in Delhi.
- The length of steel wires used (37,680 kms.) in the project is nearly equivalent to the circumference of the Earth.
- The cable stayed tower rises to a height of 126 metres, which is equal to a 43 storeyed building.
- 2.3 lakh cubic metres of concrete has been used in the project.
- The weight of the bridge (6.7 L tonnes) is equivalent to 50,000 African elephants.
- There are 424 cables for main roadway and each cable can take a weight of 900 tons.
- The bridge rests on 135 pile caps, the largest being 55 m. in length and 55 m. in breadth (size of half a football field).
- There is an Intelligent Bridge System to monitor traffic. Vehicles going over the 50 kmph. limit will be identified by an automatic system.
- The 7.7 kms distance from Mahim flyover to Love Grove Junction, Worli was covered in 35 to 38 minutes. The travel time has now been reduced to 6 minutes through the 4.7 kms. sea link
- It is expected that 7,000 to 8,000 cars will use the sea link per hour during peak hours. This will save about Rs. 260 crores of fuel every year.

Sacred Sites

Sacred Sites

Afghan or St. John's Church

St. Thomas Cathedral

✝ CHRISTIANS

Afghan or St. John's Church

The magnificent church at Colaba was built in 1847, in memory of the British soldiers who sacrificed their lives during the Sindh campaign of 1838 and the First Afghan war of 1843. It was consecrated in 1858 and is built in early classical English architecture style. The 60 m. high spire of the church stands out from its woody surroundings. Its wide Gothic arches, ornately carved walls and beautiful stained glass windows add to the beauty of the structure.

St. Thomas Cathedral

The impressive church at Fort is a fine blend of the classical and Gothic styles of architecture. It is the first English built church in Mumbai. The construction was started in 1672, but the work stopped in between and after a long gap the construction was completed. It was opened for worship on 25th December 1718. The church underwent many changes before it became the cathedral of today. It also has numerous interesting memorials and monuments.

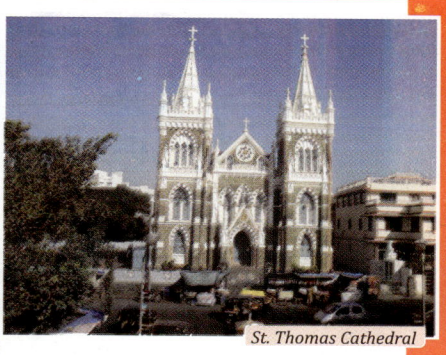

The Gloria Church

The church located at Byculla, was originally built by Portuguese in 1632. It was demolished and built in more Gothic style in 1911.

Mount Mary Church

The beautiful basilica at Bandra dedicated to the Virgin Mary is one of the most prominent and famous Roman Catholic churches of Mumbai. A week long Bandra Fair held here in the month of September, commemorating the birth of Mother Mary (8th Sept.). A large number of devotees irrespective of their faiths and religion visit the church to seek the blessings of Mother Mary. The Bandra Fair is also an important cultural event of Mumbai.

Other important churches of Mumbai are: **St. Michael's Church**, at Mahim (designed by famous architect Charles Correa, with a large hole in the roof);

St. Andrew & St. Columbia Church at Colaba and **Holy Name Cathedral** at Nathalal Parekh Road.

ॐ HINDUS & JAINS

Mumbadevi Temple

Mumbai (Mumba-ayi) is named after the Goddess Mumbadevi, the patron deity of the city. The shrine dedicated to Mumbadevi is believed to have been originally built by Koli fisherman in the 1st century B.C., on the site now occupied by Victoria or Chhatrapati Shivaji Terminus. It withstood the

Sacred Sites

Mumbadevi Temple

Mahalaxmi Temple

Mahalaxmi Temple

The temple dedicated to Mahalaxmi, the Goddess of wealth and prosperity is one of the most popular shrines of Mumbai. Set picturesquely on a rocky promontory, at the edge of the sea, the present temple was built in the 18th century. The original Mahalaxmi temple at the same spot was destroyed many centuries ago. Legend goes that while building the causeway, the great Breach Candy, between Worli and Mahim, the ferocious sea waves thwarted any such attempts. Ramji Shivji, a contractor dreamt of the Goddess Mahalaxmi, who asked him to restore the original idols submerged in the sea, if the work of building the causeway was to be completed.

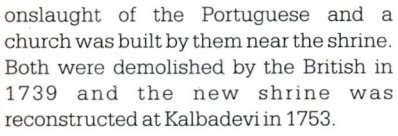

onslaught of the Portuguese and a church was built by them near the shrine. Both were demolished by the British in 1739 and the new shrine was reconstructed at Kalbadevi in 1753.

An early 18th century writer describes how the image of the Goddess in the original temple was "seated in a poor hovel upon a small altar decked with flowers, her head being three times bigger in proportion to her body". But, the present temple houses an impressive image of the Goddess, adorned with a robe and ornamented with silver crown, a glittering nose stud and a gold necklace. To the left is the idol of Goddess Annapurna seated on a peacock. In front of the temple is an image of Mumbadevi's vehicle - the tiger. Tuesday, is the main day of worship. Newly married Hindu couples visit the shrine soon after their marriage, seeking blessings from the Goddess for a happy married life.

Thus the statues of Mahalaxmi, Mahakali and Mahasaraswati were restored from the sea bed and installed in the present temple as per the wishes of the Goddess. Only then the building work of the sea-wall was successfully completed. The images of all three Goddesses are elaborately ornamented with nose rings, gold bangles and pearl necklaces. The image of Mahalaxmi is shown riding a tiger and a demon (Mahisasur) in tandem. Today, it is one of the most crowded temples of Mumbai. Thousand of devotees visit the shrine to offer prayers, flowers and coconuts. The sunset view from the temple, coupled with the voices of prayers and ringing of bells is an out of the world experience, which is to be seen to believe. The only other shrine dedicated to the Goddess

Sacred Sites

Mahalakshmi on the Indian coast is the Ashtakshmi temple at Chennai, the capital of Tamil Nadu.

Babulnath Temple

The ancient temple dedicated to Lord Shiva is located at the end of Marine Drive, on the south-east slope of Malabar Hill and is an important landmark of Mumbai. It was built in 1780, and a tall spire was added to the structure in 1900. The black stone lingam of Shiva located in the sanctum was discovered at Worli and is the chief object of worship. The sacred shrine also has idols of various other Gods and Goddesses. The temple affords a fine view of the city and can be approached through a long flight of steps as well as an elevator.

Bhuleshwar Temple

The temple dedicated to Lord Shiva also known as Bholeshwar (the Pure One), was built about 200 years ago. The temple is covered with brass plate and has a red flag adorned with representations of the sun and moon. It is believed that the lingam in the temple has miraculously risen to its present position.

Siddhi Vinayak Temple

The famous shrine dedicated to Lord Ganesha is situated at Prabhadevi. The magnificent temple was fully renovated and enlarged in 1994 and is visited by thousands of devotees, especially on Tuesday. Mumbaikars have a great respect and devotion for the holy shrine.

Siddhi Vinayak Temple

Surya Narayan Temple

The glorious temple dedicated to the Sun God is located at Surajwadi, Panjiapol Lane, Bhuleshwar. This white stone shrine was built in 1899 and is a masterpiece of architecture. At the main entrance of the shrine are the carved figures of Jay and Vijay, the celestial gatekeepers. The inner sanctum of the temple houses a majestic idol of Sun God seated on an one-wheeled chariot, drawn by a horse with seven heads. The Sun God is flanked by his two wives Prabha and Chhaya, while his lame charioteer Aruna is driving the chariot. The temple also has various sculpted images of Hindu Gods and Goddesses.

ISKCON Temple

The beautifully constructed ISKCON or Hare Rama Hare Krishna temple is located at Juhu. Peace and calm pervades at the holy shrine of worship, meditation and spiritual knowledge. The morning and evening prayers at the temple are worth attending.

Jain Temple

The beautiful Jain shrine located on B.C. Kher Marg at Malabar hill is dedicated to Adinath, the first Jain *tirthankar*. The shrine built in 1904, is constructed in marble and is a fine example of Jain temple architecture. Its walls inside are richly decorated with colourful paintings portraying the lives of the 24 Jain *tirthankars*. The first floor of the temple houses a beautifully carved black marble idol of Lord Parsvanath.

Walkeshwar Temple

It is yet another legendary Hindu shrine of Mumbai. The ancient temple near Malabar hill is believed to have been built in 1000 AD. by Silhara Kings. It was vandalised by the Portuguese fanatics in the 16th century and was beautifully rebuilt by Rama Kamthi, a wealthy Brahmin in 1715. According to a legend Lord Rama came here during his exile. Wherever Lord Rama travelled his brother provided him with a *lingam* from

Sacred Sites

Banaras for his worship every night. On this particular night, Lakshman could not reach in time for worship, thus Lord Rama made a *Shivlingam* out of sand (Waluk) and prayed. Hence the presiding deity came to be known as 'Waluk Eshwar' (Sand God) and is of great religious importance.

Banganga Temple Complex

The sacred Banganga Tank near Walkeshwar Temple, is said to have been created by Lord Rama, with a shot of his arrow to quench his thirst. Thus it came to be known as the 'Vani Teerth' (Arrow Tank). Devotees bathe in the holy water for purification.

The tank and temple here are believed to be built by teh Silhara Kings between ninth and eleventh century. There are about thirty temples, two mathas (monasteries), dharamshalas and a number of akhadas at the complex. A Hindustani Classical Music Festival is organised here by MTDC in January.

☪ MUSLIMS

Haji Ali Dargah Complex

Haji Ali, one of the most revered and spectacular shrines of the city is set on a small islet in the little bay to the north of Mahalaxmi temple. It houses the tomb of a Muslim saint, Sayed Peer Haji Ali Shah Bukhari, who died while on pilgrimage to Mecca. When the casket containing his mortal remains floated and came to rest on a rocky bed in the sea, devotees constructed the tomb and mosque at that spot. The mosque set in scenic surroundings can be approached through a causeway, which gets submerged during the high tide and the mosque appears to be floating in the sea.

Raudat Tahera

It has a marble mosque and mausoleum built by the Dawoodi Bohra Muslims in honour of their spiritual leader, the late Dr. Syedna Tahar Saifuddin. The lavishly decorated mausoleum has four silver doors and verses from the Quran are inscribed on the inner walls in gold. The unique, air-conditioned Fatemi mosque has 17 arches representing the 17 *Rakaat* prayers.

Jama Masjid

The Jama Masjid mosque is located at the Sheikh Memon Street in Kalbadevi locality. Some other important mosques are Jumma Masjid at Janjikar Street, Mosques at Bandra and Mahim etc.

Haji Ali Dargah

Sacred Sites

OTHERS

Vatcha Agiary

PARSI TEMPLES (AGIARIES)

There are several Parsi (Fire) Temples in Mumbai. These are located at Church Gate, Princess Street, New Queen's Rd., Gowalia Tank and Bandra. The Vatcha Agiary at Dadabhai Naoroji Road was built in 1881 and enshrines a sacred fire, which has been kept burning for over 300 years.

SYNAGOGUES

There are several beautiful synagogues of Bene-Israelis and Sephardic Jews in the town, housing Torah scrolls, phylacteries and prayer shawls. Some important synagogues include Kenesseth Ellyahoo Synagogue in Fort and Magen David Synagogue at Veer Jijamata Udyan, Byculla, built by the Sassoons, a Sephardic Jewish family. The Tephereth Israel Synagogue and Magen Hasidim Synagogue are located at Agripada.

GLOBAL VIPASSANA PAGODA

The huge pagoda built in the honour Lord Buddha and his teachings is set on a peninsula between Gorai creek and the Arabian Sea, near Essel World, the famous amusement park of Mumbai. Its foundation was laid in October 1997 and was completed in 11 years involving about 3.87 million man days.

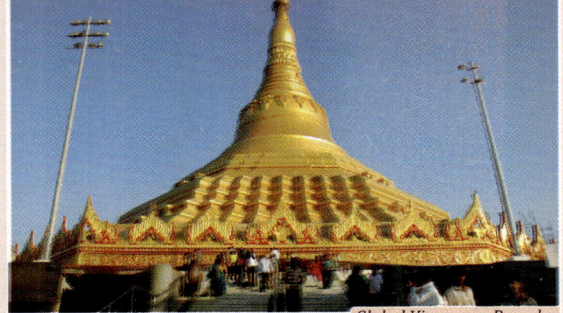

Global Vipassana Pagoda

The monument was inaugurated on February 8, 2009 by Pratibha Patil, the President of India. The modern India's biggest architectural and pilgrimage wonder is designed on the lines of the famous Shwedagon Pagoda in Yangon, Myanmar. It is built in Jodhpur sandstone using the ancient method of stone interlocking. Approximately 2.5 million tonnes of stone was used in the construction. Each stone was tested to find if it can survive the weather changes and marine environment, so that the magnificent monument lasts for at least 1,000 years. The 325 feet high structure with a diameter of 280 feet is one of the largest stone monuments in Asia and inner pillar-less dome is thrice as large as the Gol Gumbaz dome in Bijapur, which was till now considered to be the largest stone dome built without any supporting pillars. The inside of the pagoda is hollow unlike most of the pagodas around the world, which are generally solid structures. It houses original bone relics of Lord Buddha and has a gigantic meditation hall, covering an area of 6,000 sq. mtrs., where 8,000 people can practice Vipassana, an ancient Indian meditation technique. There is also a Dhamma Museum, well stocked library, multi-media presentations and seminar rooms. Vipassana is taught free of cost over here and Shri S. N. Goenka, the well known Vipassana teacher is associated with the centre.

Around Mumbai

Around Mumbai

Maheshmurti, Elephanta Caves

Elephanta Caves (9kms. by sea)

The architecturally rich island is about half an hour launch ride from the Gateway of India. It was known as Gahrapuri (fortress city) in ancient times and is famous for a series of seven magnificent rock cut caves dating from 4th to 9th century. The rock cut cave temples dedicated to Lord Shiva are set above a hill and are accessible by a long flight of steps. The Great Cave is the most impressive and is renowned for the colossal 'Maheshmurti', the 6 metre high, three headed sculpture of Lord Shiva, depicting him in one single carving as the Creator, Protector and Destroyer of the universe. On either side of the recess is a pilaster, each interestingly carved as gigantic dwarpala. On the right side of the rear cave is a series of nine massive sculpted panels, chiselled with great power and beauty on the rock walls of the cave, each composition set in a separate recess. These depict various incidents related to Lord Shiva and stories from Hindu mythology. The beauty of splendid sculptures speaks volumes of man's faith and artistic creation. Beyond the main hall, in the east wing is a open hall with a circular platform. In the court is a temple set on a high terrace. It has splendid sculptures of Shiva, Vishnu, Brahma and seven great Goddesses or divine mothers. The West Wing of the cave also has an open court and an attractive chapel.

Ambarnath (70 km.)

It is an important Hindu pilgrim centre and popular picnic spot. The town is famous for the 11th century Chalukyan temple dedicated to Lord Shiva. Ambarnath is connected by sub-urban electric trains of Central Railways from Mumbai. The road route for Mumbai - Ambarnath is via Thane, Kalyan and Ulhasnagar. S.T. buses ply from Kalyan and Ulhasnagar.

Ambarnath Temple

43

Around Mumbai

Karla Cave

Alibag (112 km.)

The home of Shivaji's admiral Angre, is a splendid bathing beach. Chaul, the ancient capital of Silhara kings and a natural port is just 15 kms. from Alibag. Chaul is known for an ancient fort, mosque and tomb of Sardar Angre. Alibag is easily approachable by road via Panvel and Pen.

Bassein Fort

It is 76.8 km by sub-urban electric train to Bassein Rd. and thence 4.8 km. by road. The 15th century Portuguese Fort is worth visiting.

Karla, Bhaja & Bedsa Caves

The Buddhist rock cut cave shrines at Karla are decorated with intricate carvings and are considered to be as beautiful as the world famous Ajanta-Ellora. The 2nd century BC Chaitya Hall of Karla is said to be the most perfect of its kind. An inscription at the entrance attributes its excavation to Bhutapal of Vaijayanti. The caves are approached by a rough path of about 2km. The nearest railhead is at Lonavala (101 km.) and thence 11 km. by road. Buses are available at Lonavala Railway Station.

The Bhaja Caves dating back to 200 BC., are set in a lush valley. Its large Chaitya cave resembles to the one at Karla. Another cave has a magnificent stilted vault. The last cave is a treasure house of rich carving. To the south of the main cave is an amazing group of 14 stupas. To the west of the caves is Lohagandh Fort, which was captured by Sivaji.

The Bedsa Caves are another set of excellent rock cut caves. One of them has a magnificent Chaitya with ribbed roof supported by 26 octagonal pillars.

Karnala Bird Sanctuary & Fort

The bird sanctuary is located 61 km. on the Mumbai - Goa road. It can be reached by State Transport buses to Panvel and thence to Karnala. Several species of birds can be seen here. An old fort nearby is quite interesting. The sanctuary has two distinct seasons for bird watching. Birds like paradise fly catchers, shama, nalabad whistling thrushes and racket tailed drongos can be seen during the monsoons (July - Sept.). While winter (Oct. - Dec.) is the time to see the blue throat, the large cuckoo and shrike etc. Panther, antelope, common langur and African monkey can also be sighted at the sanctuary.

Around Mumbai

Toy Train, Matheran

Lonavala (101 km.)
The beautiful hill resort is located on the Mumbai - Pune road. It is easily accessible by road and rail and has a large number of hotels ranging from star category to reasonably priced ones.

Khandala, is located 4 km. from here and is another charming, cool and quiet hill retreat.

Madh (90 kms.)
The Hindu pilgrim centre is one of the eight sites of the Ashta Vinayaka, which has a swayambhu (naturally formed) idol of Lord Ganesha or Vinayaka.

Matheran (110 kms.)
Matheran or the 'woodlands overhead' is aptly named as the beautiful hill resort is perched at an altitude of 800 metres in the Western Ghats and is considered to be the Asia's only pedestrian hill station. It was discovered by Hugh Malet, the collector of Thane in 1850's. Matheran is full of shady trees, mossy walks and a profusion of rare orchids. There are 33 view points, each attractive in its own way. On a clear day one can get a bird's eye view of Mumbai from the Louisa and Echo Points.

To the west of the hill is the ruined fort of Parbal, where Shivaji came to arrest an untrustworthy subordinate. It is said that Shivaji on his visit to Parbal, stopped to worship at Matheran and the path leading from One-Tree Hill to the valley is named after him. Near the path is a charming temple enshrining three naturaly formed lingams. Another shrine marks the burial place of Pisarnath, a saint of Shivaji's time. Matheran can be conveniently reached by rail. The toy train from Neral to Matheran is quite exciting. No motorised vehicles are allowed inside Matheran.

Mahabaleshwar (247 kms.)
It is one of the best known and the highest hill resort of Western India. Mahabaleshwar was developed into a charming resort by Sir John Malcolm in 1828 and has remained one of the most popular getaways for the Mumbaikars.

The beautiful hill station teeming with orchids, lilies and luscious strawberries has three silvery falls - Dhobi Falls, Chinaman Falls and Lingmala Falls. The exciting view points like Wilson Point, Babington Point, Kate Point, Elphinstone Point, Bombay Point and Arthur's Seat provide great views of the Krishna and Koyna valleys.

45

Around Mumbai

Waterfall, Mahabaleshwar

The old village of Mahabaleshwar is held sacred by the Hindus. The Panchganga temple here is said to contain five streams including the River Krishna.

Naigaon (120 kms.)
The picturesque beach resort is just 7 kms. from Alibag. One can also visit the twin Khanderi and Undheri forts from here.

Kihim (136 kms.)
The virgin Kihim beach is near Naigaon and is known for its seclusion and charm.

Pali (Sudhagad) (140 kms.)
The pilgrim centre is also a Ashta Vinayaka site. The Shri Ballaleshwar temple enshrines the swayambhu idol of Vinayaka. The Sudhagad Fort, Chhehere hot springs and Siddheswar temple are other worth visiting sites.

Shivneri (160 kms.)
It is the birthplace of Chhatrapati Shivaji. The historical fort perched atop a mammoth rocky hill is worth a visit. The Shivbai temple in the fort is built in the hollow of a Buddhist cave. The hill also has a series of Buddhist caves dating back to the 2nd and 6th centuries.

Shivneri Fort

Vaitarna Lake & Dam
The scenic lake is 122 km. by sub-urban electric train to Khardi and thence 12.8km. by road.

Vajreshwari Hot Spring / Ganeshpuri Ashram (88 km.)
The hot springs amidst scenic surroundings can be reached via suburban electric train to Bassein Rd. and thence 28.9 km. by road. or to Thane thence 33.7 km. by road. S.T. buses are available from Mumbai on Saturdays, Sundays and other holidays. There are more hot springs at the spa of Akloli.

46

Festivals

Festivals

Ganesh Chaturthi

Gudi Padwa Celebrations

Mumbai, a truly cosmopolitan metropolis is inhabited by people of all faiths, cultures and different regions. Every Indian festival is celebrated here with wholehearted zest, but the most important festival of Mumbai is undoubtedly Ganesh Chaturti.

Makar Sankranti (Jan.)
The festival is marked by kite flying competitions and exchange of sweets.

Mahashivratri (Feb./Mar.)
Worship of Lord Shiva and other religious ceremonies.

Gudi Padva (Mar./Apr.)
The Hindu Maharashtrian New Year Day, commemorates their ancient ruler Shalivahan, a potter's son who became a monarch, after overthrowing the Gupta rulers of Malwa. New ventures are started and festive spirit prevails.

Jamshedji Navroz (Mar./Apr.)
New Year for Parsees, who follow Fasli calendar.

Shivaji Jayanti (Apr./May)
Celebration of birth anniversary of Chhatrapati Shivaji.

Janmashtami (Jul./Aug.)
Birth anniversary of Lord Krishna. Earthen pots filled with curd and rice planks (Dahi Handi) are strung high up across the streets on the next day. Youngmen stand on top of one another to form a human pyramid and attempt to break the pots.

Narali Purnima or Cononut Day (Aug.)
The festival is especially important for the fishing community of the State. Coconuts are offered to the sea, to

Festivals

propitiate Varuna, the God of sky, water and celestial ocean. It marks the beginning of new fishing season.

Ramzan-Id

The Muslim festival marks the end of holy month of Ramzan.

Ganesh Chaturthi (Aug. / Sept.)

It is Mumbai's most important and colourful festival. During the 10 day celebrations Lord Ganesh is worshipped in millions of homes. Larger than life images of Lord Ganesha are installed and beautiful decorations are made. The images are bedecked with flowers and sandalwood paste or turmeric and flowers, betel leaves and betel nuts are offered in worship in a ceremony, which is performed for nine days. On the last day of the festival, colourful processions are taken out, carrying the images of Ganesha, which are immersed in the sea. Mumbai is the best place to see this festival.

Pateti (Aug.)

The Parsi New Year celebrated by the Shahenshahi section of the community, marks the migration of the Parsis from Persia to India.

Mt. Mary's Feast (Sept.)

The feast in the honour of Our Lady of the Mount is celebrated with great solemnity at St. Mary's Church, Bandra. A week long Bandra fair is held during this time, attracting a large number of people.

Navratri (Sept./Oct.)

A 10 day festival. Nine nights are spent in worship and entire Mumbai swings to the rhythm of Garba and Raas dances of Gujarati community.

Dussehra (Sept./Oct.)

It marks the victory of Lord Rama over the demon king Ravanna. It is also the best time to see the Dindi and Kala folk dances of Maharashtra. Rural theatre and Tamasha shows can also be seen.

Diwali (Oct./Nov.)

Festival of Lights. Start of New Year and opening of new accounts. Worshipping of Goddess Laxmi.

Id-uz-Zuha (Bakr-Id)

It commemorates Abraham's sacrifice of his son.

Christmas (25th Dec.)

The Christian festival ushers in the season of goodwill, greetings and festive shopping.

TOURIST FESTIVALS

Banganga Festival

The musical festival is organised by MTDC, every year at Banganga Tank on Malabar Hill in January.

Elephanta Festival

Elephanta Festival

MTDC holds this annual classical dance and music festival in February at the historic Elephanta Islands.

Kala Ghoda

The arts and crafts festival is held every Sunday from Nov. to Dec. on K.Dubash Marg.

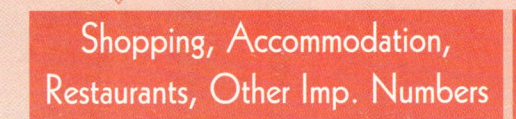

Shopping, Accommodation, Restaurants, Other Imp. Numbers

Shopping

Shopping is indeed a memorable experience in this commercial nerve centre of the country. One can pick fine goods at throw-away prices from temporary road-side stalls or visit posh emporias and boutiques. The bustling bazars of Mumbai cater to every demand of the shopper's. One may browse through endless list of products, ranging from from house hold articles, textiles and leather-ware to engineering goods and electronic gadgets. The variety and pricing are simply mindboggling.

THINGS TO BUY

Textiles : Mumbai is a traditional textile centre of India. A range of handwoven and handprinted silks and cottons as well as the trendiest new materials can be purchased here. Some of the fabric worth purchasing are — the Pune saree in vibrant checks, stripes or woven border ; the Khand blouse pieces and hand woven specialities from Bhiwandi. The Surat *bandhni* (tie-dye material) are available in wide range of colours and patterns. Other fabrics available here are *Aurangabad himroo*, cotton brocade woven in gold and silver threads ; Block printed fabric from Ahmadabad; fine muslin from Sanganer and Gujarat's *Kalamkari* work.

Garments : Mumbai is India's fashion capital. One can purchase fine garments at reasonable prices from pavement markets as well as branded and designer garments at high priced plush airconditioned stores and boutiques.

Handicrafts : The city is a treasure trove of traditional handicrafts from all over the country. The main attractions are attractive furnitures from Sankheda in Gujarat ; Applique toys, wall hangings, bedspreads, cushion covers, dhurries, ceramics etc. from Kachcch ; and carved brass and copper pots, and pottery of Maharashtra etc.

Leather : India's finest finished leather goods are produced in Mumbai. Excellent shoes, bags, wallets, jackets, coats, belts and briefcases etc. can be purchased here. The traditional Kolhapuri chappals are also very popular.

Diamonds : Mumbai is also an important centre for Diamond trade and exquisite diamond jewellery can be purchased here.

Shopping

MAIN SHOPPING AREAS

Colaba Causeway
It is one of the finest shopping areas of Mumbai. A wide range of garments, fabrics, footwear and leather accessories can be purchased here.

Mereweather Road
It is located behind the famous Taj Mahal Hotel and is known for exquisite carpets.

Fort
The area around Flora Fountain specialises in various products like cameras, watches, stationary items and book-shops etc.

Fashion Street
This market of export surplus and reject garments is located just opposite to the famous Mumbai Gymkhana. It is a great place for shopping at an unbelievable price. Bargaining is a must overhere. Nearby are famous landmarks like Metro Cinema and Dhobi Talao.

Crawford Market

Mahatma Jyotiba Phule Market or Crawford Market
The market located in the lanes of Mohammad Ali Road was constructed in 1867, through the unflagging drive of Arthur Crawford, the Municipal Commissioner of Bombay. This large Flemish-Moorish style market building is the best place to enjoy noisy, bustling, quaintly picturesque charms of the Indian bazar. The market covers an area of 60,200 sq. mts. and has a large central hall and two wings, where fresh fruits, vegetables, mutton, fish and other provision stalls are located.

The main building is constructed from coarse Kurla rubble with coignes of Porbandar stone enlivened by warm redstone from Bassein. In the central hall is a drinking fountain set up by Sir Cowasjee Jehangir. There is also a 39 metres high clock tower. The panels above the three gateways are adorned with sculpted scenes showing, one of a group of beautiful women representing the principal rivers of India, done by Lockwood Kipling; another of an idealised vision of agricultural life, with peasants and a helpful dog standing among stony wheat sheaves.

Fabric markets of the city are also centred around this area. Mangaldas Market, is a wholesale market for both synthetics and cottons, while Mohtaa and Mulji Jetha Markets are known for imported yarns.

Kalbadevi
The densely populated area is one of the busiest areas of commercial activity in India and is probably one of its kind in the country. A maze of interconnected lanes and bylanes comprise this area which is indeed a shopper's paradise. One can get goods ranging from ordinariness of cotton textiles to the opulence of diamonds. It has some of the oldest and finest markets of Mumbai.

Jhaveri Bazar : It is known for exquisite gold and diamond jewellery. City's major jewellery stores have there main branches in this market. The silver market is located nearby at Pydhonie.

Mulji Jetha : It is considered to be the largest textile market in Asia.

Dawa Bazar : It is known for pharmaceutical goods. Stationary and booksellers mart is nearby.

Lohar Chawl : It is famous for hardware and electrical goods.

The area near Mumbadevi Temple is known for finished goods in brass, aluminium and copper. Other specialised places are — For yarn and dyes near

Shopping

Tambakata; crockery, cutlery and pottery at Lohar street and Dana Bunder for food grains.

Mohammed Ali Road
For itars (locally made perfumes), embroidery and zari work.

Bhuleshwar Area and Chor Bazar
Jain Gujarati Bhuleshwar area is a good place to buy ethnic utensils of copper and brass.

Chor Bazar, the second hand market is a collector's delight. The stalls here are stocked with amazing antique items, decorative pieces, lamp-shades etc. Audio systems, televisions and other electronic items are also available, but beware of being duped.

Warden Rd./Bhulabhai Desai Rd.
The posh area starting from Haji Ali end upto Kemp's Corner is studded with exquisite boutiques, show-rooms and shopping centres. Other upmarket shopping arcades are at Oberoi Towers, Nariman Point and Taj Mahal Hotel, Apollo bunder. There are exclusive showrooms and boutiques located here.

World Trade Centre, Cuffe Parade
Visit for excellent handicraft and handloom items at various State Emporias. One can be assured about the quality of goods at these emporias, although the prices are on the higher side.

Dadar
The centrally located Dadar is very popular among the middle class. You can buy almost anything. It is worth visiting especially during the festive season. The Gandhi Bazar is well known for fabric shopping. Dadar also has Mumbai's biggest wholesale flower market.

Bandra
Bandra, the 'Queen of Sub-urbs' is home to several important cine stars, industrialists etc. The Linking Road connecting Bandra and Khar is a famous shopping belt and is rated as one of the most popular shopping areas of Mumbai. Most large shops of Mumbai have there branches overhere. Shopping at the busy road-side stalls is fun and bargaining is a must. Elco Arcade on Hill Rd. is other popular shopping area.

Ulhas Nagar
Popularly called as the USA of Mumbai, it is the Mecca of 'copies'. Everything is copied here with great perfection. One can enjoy shopping the duplicates of branded items at shoe-string budget over here.

53

Shopping

STATE EMPORIUMS

Central Cottage Industries Emporium, 34, C. S. Marg, Nr. Gateway of India, Colaba

Gangotri, U.P. Export Corpn. World Trade Centre, Cuffe Parade

Black Partridge, Haryana Govt. Emporium, Air India Bldg., Nariman Pt.

Gurjari, Gujarat Govt. Emporium Khetan Bhavan, J. Tata Rd.

Himachal Pradesh Handicrafts Emp., World Trade Centre, Cuffe Parade

Jammu & Kashmir Govt. Emp. World Trade Centre, Cuffe Parade

Kairali, Kerala Govt. Emporium Nirmal Bldg., Nariman Point

Khadi & Village Industries Emporium 286, Dr. D.N. Road

Mrignayanee, M. P. Govt. Emporium World Trade Centre, Cuffe Parade

Rajasthali, Rajasthan Govt. Emporium 230, Dr. D. N. Road

Trimurti, Maharashtra S. S. I. Dev. Corpn., 30 World Trade Centre

SHOPPING MALLS

Atria Shopping Mall, Lovegrove Junction, Dr. Annie Besant Rd., Nr. Planetarium, Worli

CR 2 Shopping Mall, Nariman Point

Crossroads, Near Haji Ali, Tardeo

Galleria Shopping Mall, Hiranandani Garden, Powai

Grand Hyatt Plaza Off Western Express Highway, Santacruz (E) 66761234

High Street Phoenix, 462 Senapati Bapat Marg, Lower Parel.......................2496-4307

Infiniti Shopping Mall, New Link Road, Oshiwara, Andheri (W) (Best place for branded stores and entertainment for entire family)

Inorbit Shopping Mall, Mindspace, New Link Rd., Malad (W) 56777999

Oberoi Mall, Oberoi Garden City, off Western Express Highway, International Business Park, Goregaon (E).

Orchid City Centre, 265 Bellasis Road, Mumbai Central...........................66104300

R-Mall, L. B. S. Marg, Mulund (W)5555-4143

BOOKS

Crosswords, Mohammed Bhai Mansion, Kemps Corner, N.S. Patkar Mrg 23842001

Granth.com, 270, Citi Center, Swami Vivekanand Rd., Goregaon (W)....28768989

Granth.com, 30/A, H.M. House, Juhu Tara Rd. Santacruz (W)........26609327/26609337

IMAX Adlabs, Link Road, Bhakti Park, Wadala 24036595

Landmark, Basement, Palladium, Senapati Bapat Marg, Lower Parel...............64575323

Landmark, New Link Rd., Infiniti Mall, Andheri (W) 26396010

Nalanda, Taj Mahal Palace, Colaba 22022514

New & Second Hand Bookstore, Kalbadevi Rd., Dhobi Talao 22013314

Nirmal Lifestyle Mall, 1st Floor Mulund (W) 25934627

Oxford Bookstore, Apeejay House, 3 Dinsha Vachha Rd, Churchgate .56364477

CLOTHES

For trendy garments and accessories at throwaway prices visit Fashion Street, between Cross and Azad Maidans, near the famous Metro cinema.

The pavement stalls at Linking Road, near Waterford Rd., at Bandra is yet another place for buying cheap and good quality clothes, but has to be good at bargaining at places like Fashion Street and pavement stalls at Linking Road. There are also posh showrooms on both sides of Linking Road. Kemps Corner, Warden Road, Breach Candy and Napean Sea Road are some other places to buy garments and accessories in style.

HANDICRAFTS/ANTIQUES

Art India, 241, Princess Street

Colorama Exports,

Hotel Oberoi Towers, Nariman Point

India Carpets, 55, Oberoi Shopping Centre, Nariman Pt.

India House No. 4, Kemps Corner

Indian Art Corner, 66/9 Mutton St.

Mughal Art Co.

Florence House, Mereweather Rd.

Nizam Art & Jewels, Meherabad Bldg., Warden Rd.

Accommodation

ACCOMMODATION

5 STAR DELUXE

Grand Hyatt Mumbai, Off Western Express Highway, Santa Cruz (East) 66761234
Hyatt Regency Mumbai,
Sahar Airport Road 66961234
Intercontinental The Grand Mumbai
Sahar Airport Rd, Andheri (E)............. 66992222
ITC Grand Central Sheraton & Towers,
287, Dr B Ambedkar Rd., Parel............ 24101010
ITC Maratha - The Luxury Collection,
Sahar, Andheri (E)................................ 28303030
JW Marriot, Juhu Tara Rd. 6693300
Leela Kempinski,
Opp. Intl. Airport, Sahar 66911234
Le Royal Meridien
Sahar Airport Rd, Andheri (E) 28380000
Novotel Mumbai,
Balraj Sahani Marg, Juhu Beach......... 66934444
Retreat,
Madh-Marve Rd., Malad (W).............. 28813500
Sun-n-Sand, 39/2, Juhu Beach........... 66938888
Taj Lands End, Lands End,
Bandstand, Bandra (W) 66681234
Taj Mahal Palace & Tower,
Apollo Bunder, Colaba........................ 66653366
Taj President,
90 Cuffe Parade, Colaba 66650808
The Oberoi, Nariman Point 66325757
Trident, Nariman Point..................... 66324343

5 STAR

Inter Continental, Marine Drive 39879999
Marine Plaza, 29 Marine Drive.......... 22851212
Marriott Executive, Near Chinmayanand Ashram, Powai 66928888
Orchid, Nehru Rd., Vile Parle (E)........ 26164040
Ramada Plaza Palm Grove,
Juhu Beach 26112323
Sahara Star,
Mumbai Airport, Vile Parle (E) 26156660
Sea Princess,
969 Juhu Tara Rd., Juhu Beach 26611111
Sea Rock Sheraton,
Land's End, Bandra.............................. 26425454
The Resort,
Aksa Beach, Malad(W)....................... 28808888

4 STAR

Ambassador, Veer Nariman Rd.,
Church Gate 22041131
Bawa International, Nr. Domestic Airport,
Ville Parle (E)....................................... 26113636

Best Western The Emerald,
Juhu Tara Rd. 67144000
Comfort Inn Heritage,
Opp. Gloria Church, Byculla (E) 23714891
Fariyas, 25, Off Arthur Bunder Rd.,
Colaba... 22042911
Kohinoor Continental,
Andheri (E)... 28209999
Mirador, 131, New Link Rd.,
Chakala, Andheri (E) 66495000
Ramee Guestline,
Kohinoor Rd., Dadar (E) 24115353
Ramee Guestline, Juhu, A.B.N. Rd. Juhu,
Vile Parle (W) 66935555
Shalimar, August Kranti Mg. 66641000
West End, 45 New Marine Lines........ 40839121

3 STAR

Airlink, 75, Santacruz Airport 67267000
Ajanta, 8 Juhu Tara Rd....................... 26607878
Astoria,
4, J.Tata Rd., Church Gate.................. 66541234
Avion, Nehru Rd., Vile Parle (E) 26116958
Balwas International,
Bellasis Rd., Mumbai Central 23081481
Bawa Continental,
Juhu Tara Rd., Juhu 26117503
Centre Point, Turbhe Naka,
Vashi, Navi Mumbai 27683311
Citizen, 960 Juhu Beach 66932525
Columbus, Nanda Patkar Mg.,
Vile Parle (E) 26184357
Damji's, Vile Parle (E)........................ 26152921
Days Inn, Sec.-19,
Vashi, Navi Mumbai 27800404
Excutive Enclave, Pali Hill,
Bandra (W) 66969000
Godwin, 41 Garden Rd., Colaba........ 22872050
Gordon House,
Apollo Bunder, Colaba 22871122
Heritage Comfort Inn,
Sant Sawta Marg, Byculla.................. 23714891
Kohinoor Park,
Opp. Siddhivinayak Temple,
Prabhadevi 24385555
Kumaria Presidency,
Opp. International Airport 28342025
Nagina,
Dr. B A Rd., Byculla 23717799
Parle International
Agarwal Mkt., Vile Parle (E) 26102122
Ramee International
757, S.V. Rd. Khar (W) 26485421

55

Accommodation

Rang Sharda, Bandra Reclamation,
Bandra (W) 26438121
Regency, 73, Napean Sea Rd. 66571234
Regent, R.K. Mandir Rd., Andheri (E)28342020
Rodas, Hiranandani Gardens,
Powai 66936969
Royal Inn, Linking Rd., Khar (W) 26495151
Royal Garden, Juhu Tara Rd. 26603516
Shalimar, August Kranti Mg. 66641000
Shubhangan, 21st Rd., Khar (W) 40012340
Suba Palace, Apollo Bunder, Colaba.22020636
Suncity Residency, Andheri (E).........28306131
Sun-n-Sheel, Andheri Kurla Rd.,
Andheri (E)...28238811
Supreme Heritage, Sec19, Vashi,
New Mumbai.......................................27650580
The Residence, 16/17, Saki Vihar Rd.,
Powai 28575000
Transit, Off Nehru Rd., Vile Parle (E)..66930761
Tunga International, Opp. Mahakali
Caves Rd., Andheri (E).......................66921212

2 STAR
Atithi, 77, Nehru Rd., Vile Parle (E) 26116124
Bawa Regency, G.P. Rd., Dadar (E) ...40498383
Blue Ballerina,
Erangal Beach, Madh-Marve Rd. 65932844
Boutique Bawa Suites,
Linking Rd., Khar (W)..........................67397000
Broadway, Sion - Trombay Rd. 25280293
Diplomat, Apollo Bunder....................22021661
Executive Enclave, Pali Hill, Bandra66969000
Galaxy,
Prabhat Colony, Santacruz (E)..........26185035
Hiltop, 43 Pochkanwal Rd., Worli 66502000
Host Inn International,
Marol Naka, Andheri (E)......................28360105
Juhu Residency, Juhu Tara Rd..........26184546
Kemp's Corner, August Kranti Mg....23634646
Laxmi International, Goregaon (W).28722777
Linkway, Linking Road., Khar 26496341
Metro International,
Sakinaka Jn., Andheri (E)...................66941010
Metro Palace, 355, Ramdas Nayak Rd.,
Bandra (W) 26427022
Midland, J. N. Rd., Santacruz (E) 26110413
Parkway, Ranade Road., Dadar.........24453561
Residency, 26, Gunbow St., Fort 22625525
Royal Orchid, A.N.G.Acharya Mg.,
Chembur..25201234
Sea Side, 39/2, Juhu Beach................67393700

Suresha, Chakala, Andheri (E)..........28232323
Tirupati, Marol-Maroshi Rd.,
Andheri (E)..28370203

1 STAR
Krishna Palace,
Sleater Rd., Nana Chk 23894141
Park-Lane, Phalke Rd. Dadar 24114741
Rajdoot, 19, J.Bunder Rd.,
Cotton Green 23714444
Sea Green, 145, Marine Drive...........22822294
Sea Green South,
145/A, Marine Drive 22821613

STANDARD
Abbott, Vashi, New Mumbai............27826677
Accord,
Nehru Rd., Santacruz (E)....................26103464
Airlines International, Yoga Ins. Rd.,
Prabat Colony, Santacruz (E).............26160714
Airport Intl., Vile Parle (E) 26182222
Amigo, Shivaji Park, Dadar 24463530
Apollo, Landsdowne Rd., Colaba......22873312
Ascot, 38 Garden Rd.,
Colaba Causeway 22872105
Atlantic, 18/B, Tara Rd., Juhu............26602440
Avon Ruby, 87, Naigaon Cross Rd.,
Dadar (E) 24114591
Bandra Residency, Bansidhar Bhuvan,
Bandra Station (W) 26456032
Chateau Windsor, Church Gate 22044455
Classic, 31, S.V. Rd., Above Central Bank,
Santacruz (W) 26491456
Grand, Srott Rd., Ballard Estate 66580500
Gulistan, 196, Lamington Rd. 23081461
Highway Inn, Andheri-Kurla Rd.......26847071
Hill View, Worli Naka 24961858
Intercontinental Marin Drive,
135, Marin Drive 39879999
Ista, Dr A B Rd., Worli 24973408
Jayshree, 197 Dayaldas Rd.,
Vile Parle (E)..67894000
Jewel of Chembur,
Nr. Natraja Cinema, Chembur 25275000
Juhu, Juhu Beach................................66938230
Juhu Plaza, 39/2, Juhu Beach 66959600
Karan Palace,
Sonawala Rd., Goregaon (E) 26861615
Landmark Fort, 249, P.D. Mello Rd.,
Near G.P.O., C.S.T...............................30222300
Legend, Plot No. 53, Nehru Road,
Santacruz (E) 26102000

Restaurants

Manali, 74, Manchhubhai Road,
Malad (E)...28899810
Midtown Pritam,
20-B, Pritam Estates, Dadar (E)..........24145555
New Castle,
355, Linking Road, Khar (W) 26480483
Park Plaza Royal Palms, 169,
Aarey Milk Col., Goregaon (E)............28795000
Regency Inn, 18, Lansedowne House,
M.B. Marg, Colaba...............................22821630
Ritz, 5 J. Tata Rd., Church Gate 22820141
Royal Inn, Opp. Khar Tele. Exch.
Linking Road, Khar (W).......................26495151
Royal Orchid, N G Acharya Marg.,
Chembur...25201234
Sahara Star, Batra Hospitality Pvt. Ltd.,
Mumbai Airport...................................26156660
Sahil,
J.B. Behram Mg., Mumbai Cent.........23081421
Saigal Guest House,
S V Rd., Goregaon (W)........................28722477
Samrat,
Nr. Railway Station, Khar (W) 26464819
Sea Lord, 167, P.D'Mello Rd. 22615785
Sea Palace, 26, P.J. Ramchandani Marg,
Apollo Bunder.....................................22841828
Sharda,
573/A, JSS Rd., Chirabazar 22058217
Shelley's, 30, P.J. Ramchandani Marg,
Colaba Seaface....................................22840229
Silver Inn, Marol Maroshi Rd.,
Near Fire Brigade, Andheri (E) 29206911
Singh's International, Khar (W) 26496806
Supreme, 4 Panday Rd., Colaba 22185623
Strand, P.J. Ramchandani Marg,
Apollo Bunder Road............................22882222

RESTAURANTS

CHINESE

Cafe Sea Side, Band Stand, Bandra
China Gate, 155, Waterfield Rd., Bandra (W)
China Pavillion, 4 Bungalows, Andheri (W)
Chinese Room, AK Mrg., Kemps Corner
Dynasty, SV Rd.. Santacruz (W)
Great Wall, Thakur Cplx. W Exp., Kandivli
Golden Dragon, Taj Mahal Hotel
Hong Kong, Apollo Bunder Rd., Colaba
Ming Yang, TajLands End, Bandra Bnd Stnd
Pearl of the Orient,
  Ambassador Hotel.., Church Gate
Sampan, Holiday Inn, Juhu

COASTAL

Ankur, Tamarind Lane, Fort
Fresh Catch, Kotnis Marg, Mahim
Gajalee, Vile Parle (E)
Golden Crown,
  August Kranti Mrg., Kemps Corner
Highway Gomantak,
  Gandhi Ngr., Bandra (E)
Ratnagiri, Lokhandwala Cplx., Andheri (W)
Sindhudurg, RK Vaidya Rd. Dadar (W)
Shamiana, Juhu Rd., Santacruz (W)
Soul Fry, Pali Mala Rd., Bandra (W)

CONTINENTAL & MULTICUISINE

Cafe Royal, Oberoi Towers
Gaylord, Nariman Rd., Church Gate
Gossip, Worli Sea Face
Jewel of India, Discovery of India Bldg.,
  Dr. A. Besant Rd., Worli
Kobe, Hughes Rd.
La Rottisserie, The Oberoi
Mauriya, Opp. RTO., S.V. Rd. Khar
Ocean Side, Centaur Juhu
Oriental, Centaur Airport
The Top, Ambassador Hotel
Yoko, S.V. Rd., Santa Cruz
Zodiac Grill, Taj Intercontinental

GUJARATI / RAJASTHANI

Chetana, Opp. Jehangir Art Gallery
Gautam's Thali, Kalbadevi Rd.
Kichedi Samrat, V.P. Rd., C.P. Tank
Panchavati Gaurav, Behind Bombay Hosp.
Purohit's, V. Nariman Rd., Church Gate
Rajdhani, Nr. Crawford Mkt.
Samrat, J.T. Rd., Church Gate
Siddhartha, S.V. Rd. Bandra (W)
Society, Veer Nariman Rd.
Status, Nariman Pt.
Thackers Veg., 116/118, 1st Marine Street
Thackers Caterers, Chowpatty

PUNJABI / MUGHLAI

Aladin, Opp. Regal Cinema, Colaba
Amantran, Worli Naka
Aram, Government Clny, Bandra (W)
Asian, Asian Century Bazar, Worli
Bakers, 3 New Marine Lines
Balaji, Hill Rd., Bandra (W)
Bay View, Gorai Rd., Borivali (W)
Bay View, Citizen Hotel, Juhu Beach
Cafe Bandra, Hill Rd., S.V. Rd.

Other Important Numbers

Cafe City, A. Besant Rd, Worli Naka
Copper Chimney, Worli
Delhi Darbar, SBS Rd., Colaba
Dwarka, NM Rd., Fort
Food Inn, Lokhandwala Cmpx, Andheri (W)
Foodland, Sainath Rd., Malad (W)
Gazebo, Linking Rd. Bandra (W)
Great Punjab, Linking Rd., Bandra (W)
Green House, Nehru Rd, Vile Parle (E)
Holiday Inn, Juhu Beach
Indian Summer, V. Nariman. Rd., Church Gate
Kandahar,
The Oberoi, Nariman Pt.
Khyber, MG Rd., Kalaghoda
Kamath's Vaibhav, M.G. Rd., Fort
Sheetal Bukhara, Off Linking Rd.
Signature, 7 Bungalows, Versova
West End, 45 New Marine Lines

SOUTH INDIAN

Bharat Coffe House, G.K Mg., Worli
Kamath Vaibhav, M.G. Rd., Fort
Kanchi, AK Rd., Andheri (E)
Madras Bhuvan, Kalbadevi Rd.
Palms, The Oberoi, Nariman Pt.
Ramakrishna, Nehru Rd., Vile Parle
Sadanand Coffee House, Worli Sea Face
Sagar, 1st Marine St.
Satkar, Opp. Churchgate Stn.
Savera, S. V. Rd., Andheri (W)
South Indian Concerns Ltd., Matunga,
Udipi Bhavan, Bengal Chem, Worli
West End, 45 New Marine Lines
Woodside Inn, Opp. Regal Cinema

PUBS / DISCOTHEQUES

Club Abyss, Bandra
Club 9, Khar
Cyclone, Andheri (E)
Earthquake, Tardeo
Fashion Bistro, CST
Headquarters, Colaba
J49, Juhu
Rasna Pub, Church Gate
The Boulevard, Hotel Orchid
The Ghetto, Mahalaxmi

HOSPITALS

Bhagwati, Borivali.............................28932461
Bhakti Vedanta, Mira Rd..................28459888
Bhatia, Tardeo 56660000
Bombay, New Marine Lines 22067676
Breach Candy, Warden Rd. 23672888
Cooper, Vile Parle 26207254
ENT, Fort 22042526
G.T., Dhobi Talao 22621468
Ghatkopar Hindu Sabha 25094452
Hinduja, Mahim..................................24451515
Holy Spirit, Andheri (E) 28248500
Homeopathic, Vile Parle (E) 26201127
INHS Asvini, Navy Nagar
J.J., Byculla 23739400
Jaslok, Peddar Rd..............................56573333
K.E.M., Parel 24136051
Kasturba, Sane Guruji Mg................23083901
Lilavati, Bandra Reclm......................26405119
Lotus, Juhu 26207352
L.T.M.G, Sion 24076381
Mangal Anand, Chembur..................25224845
Masina, Byculla 23776656
Muktabai Municipal, Ghatkopar 25126088
Nanavati, Vile Parle (W) 26144712
Parsi, Kemps Corner.........................23633641
Poddar Ayurvedic, Worli 24933533
Prince Aly Khan, Mazgaon 23777800
Rajawadi, Ghatkopar 25094149
Saifee, Charni Rd. 55570111
S. K. Patil (Piramal), Malad 28894381
St. George, CST, Fort.......................22620244
Tata Memorial, Parel 24170001
Veer Savarkar, Mulund 25686225
Wadia Children, Parel 24129786

FOREIGN MISSIONS

Afghanistan, 115 Walkeshwar Rd. ...23633777
Austria, Bandra (E) 22874758
Australia,
Maker Tower 'E', Cuffe Parade 22181071
Brazil, 33 New Marine Lines............22002256
Bahrain, Cuffe Parade.......................22185856
Belgium, 1 M.L. Dhanukar Mg. 23521602
Canada, Nariman Pt. 22876027
Costa Rica, Dr. D.N. Rd. Fort 22040351
Czech Rep., 5 Peddar Rd.................23518456
Denmark, Ballard Estate 22614462
Finland, 40 A Peddar Rd. 23863371
France, N.G. Cross Rd, Off Peddar Rd 66694000
Germany, Hoechst Hse, Nariman Pt. 22832422
Greece, Opera House, Mathew Rd....26607852
Iceland, Sir P.M. Rd. 22871931
Indonesia, Cumabala Hill 23800940

Other Important Numbers

Iran, Napean Sea Rd. 23631029
Rep. of Ireland, Apollo Bunder..........66355635
Israel, Deshmukh Mg., Peddar Rd. 23862794
Italy, 72 G. Deshmukh Mg..................23874071
Japan,
Dahanukar Mg., Off Peddar Rd. 23517101
Madagascar, Ismail Bldg., Fountain 22046735
Malaysia, 7 Homji Street 22660056
Mauritius, Mittal Tower, Nariman Pt.22845466
Netherlands, Marine Lines................22016750
Norway, Nathelal Parekh Mg 22841368
Oman, Nariman Point.........................22876037
Peru, 6 K. Dubash Mg. 22871089
Philippines, 215 Nariman Point........22024792
Poland, 36, Ridge Rd, Malabar Hill....23633863
Qatar, Bajaj Bhawan, Nariman Point 22027192
Russia, 42 Napean Sea Rd. 23633627
Saudi Arabia, Cuffe Parade...............22187768
Singapore, 230 Nariman Pt. 22043205
Spain, 6, K Dubash Rd. 22871089
Sri Lanka, Fort 22045861
Sweden, Prabhadevi 24902161
Switzerland, Nariman Pt. 22884563
Thailand, Bhulabhai Desai Rd. 22821628
Turkey, Vile Parle (E) 66988000
U.A.E., Cuffe Parade, Colaba............56345566
United Kingdom,
Maker Chamber IV, Nariman Pt 22830517
U.S.A., 78 Bhulabhai Desai Rd...........23633611

TOURS & TRAVELS

Ambassador Travels,
A S Marathe Rd., Prabhadevi 24371550
American Express,
Shivaji Marg, Colaba 22048291
Breeze Travels,
Raheja Chmbs, 617 Nariman Pt. 22833804
Citizen Travels,
Sitaram Bldg., Crawfor Mkt.................23470150
Cox & Kings
16 Bank Street, Fort............................22073066
Raja Rani Travels,
L J Rd., Mahim 24467676
Travel Corp. of India
Chandramukhi, Nariman Pt...............22027120
Thomas Cook,
Cooks Building, Dr. DN Road 22048556
Thomas Cook,
Sion Trombay Rd, Chembur 25291355
Transway International 26146854

RITCO Travels,
Cama Bldg., 26 Dalal St. 66333790
Sita Travels
308 Town Centre, Andheri (E) 56492000

TOURIST INFORMATION

Maharashtra Tourism Dev. Corpn.
Madame Cama Rd. 22852182
Dom. Airport Counter 26149200
Extn. 354
Intnl. Airport Counter 28325331
Extn.3253
MTDC Booth Apollo Bunder 22841877
Garhwal Mandal Vikas Nigam,
Opp. LIC Bldg.Madam Cama Rd........22843197
Govt. of India Tourist Office
123 M.K. Rd., Church Gate 22074333
Govt. of Tamil Nadu Tourist Office
Royal GraceMg2, Dadar (E)................24110118
India Tourism Mumbai
1st Flr, W Rly. Bldg.,Church gate 22093229
M.P. State Tourism Dev. Corp.
World Trade Centre,Cuffe Parade.......22187603
Tourism Corp. of Gujarat Ltd.
Dhanraj Mahal, Apollo Bunder 22024925
U.P. State Tourism Dev. Corp.
World Trade Centre,Cuffe Parade.......22185458
Australian Tourist Commission,
210 Tardeo Rd. 23511523
Govt. of Dubai,
Bajaj Bhvn., Nariman Pt. 22833497
Malaysia Tourism Promotion Bd,
123 Jolly Mkr Chmb Nar. Pt. 66352085

IMPORTANT SERVICES

Regional Passport Office,
216 Manish Comm Ctr, Worli............24931555
Passport (Thane Branch) 25349008
SEBI (Greivance Cell) ....22850451 - 56
RTO Offices,
Andheri.........................26362252 / 26319821
Worli 24935857
Thane 25343580
Traffic Police Control Room 24937755
Traffic Helpline Numbers.................3040 3040
Fire Brigade,
Control Room, Mumbai ....101 / 23085991
Contol Room, Thane................101 / 25331600
Control Room, Vashi ....102 / 27660101
Foreigner's Regional Registration Office,
Annexe Bldg.No.2, CID, 3rd Flr.,
Sayed Badruddin Rd........................226204466

59

Thane

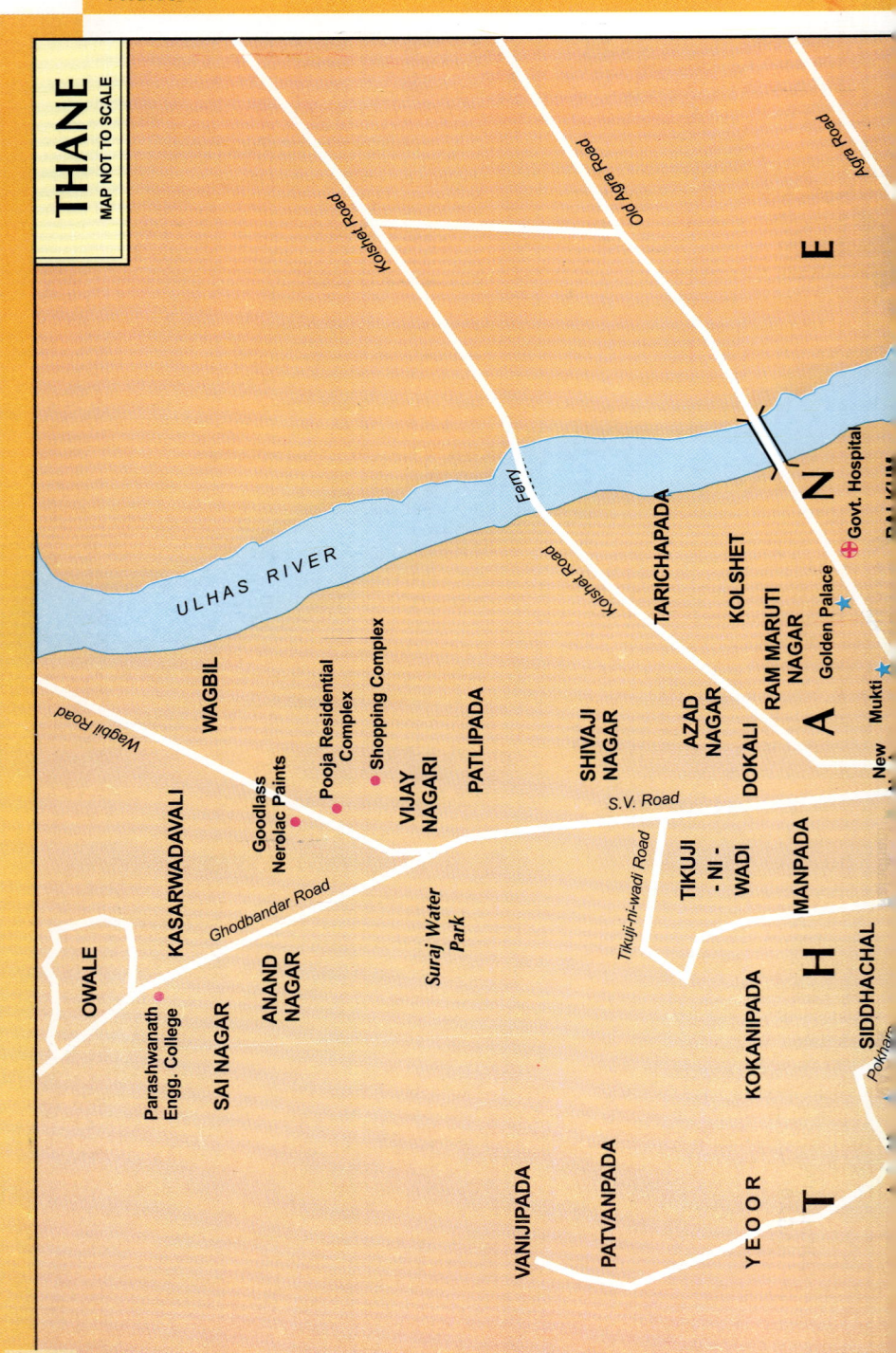

Thane

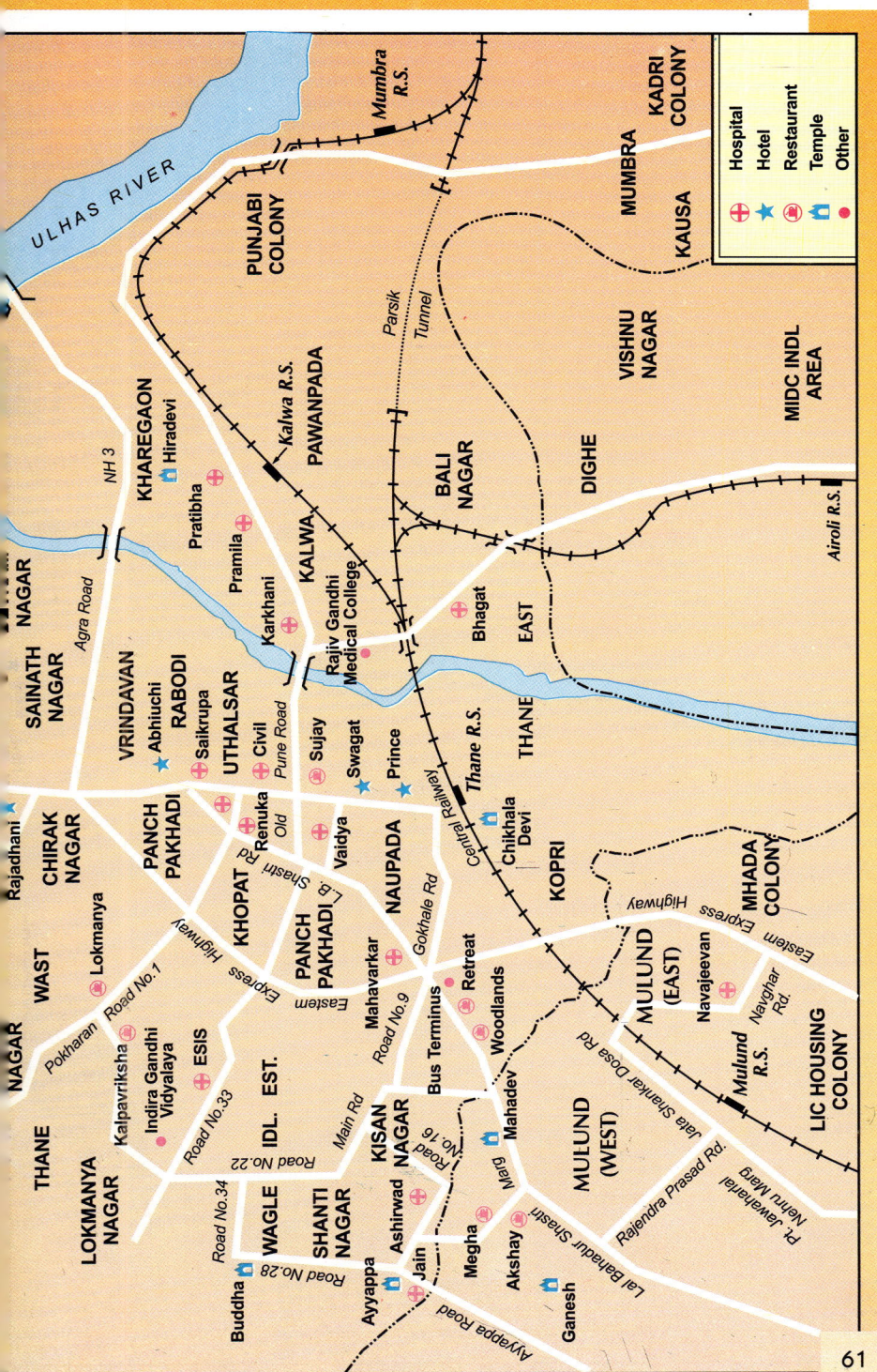

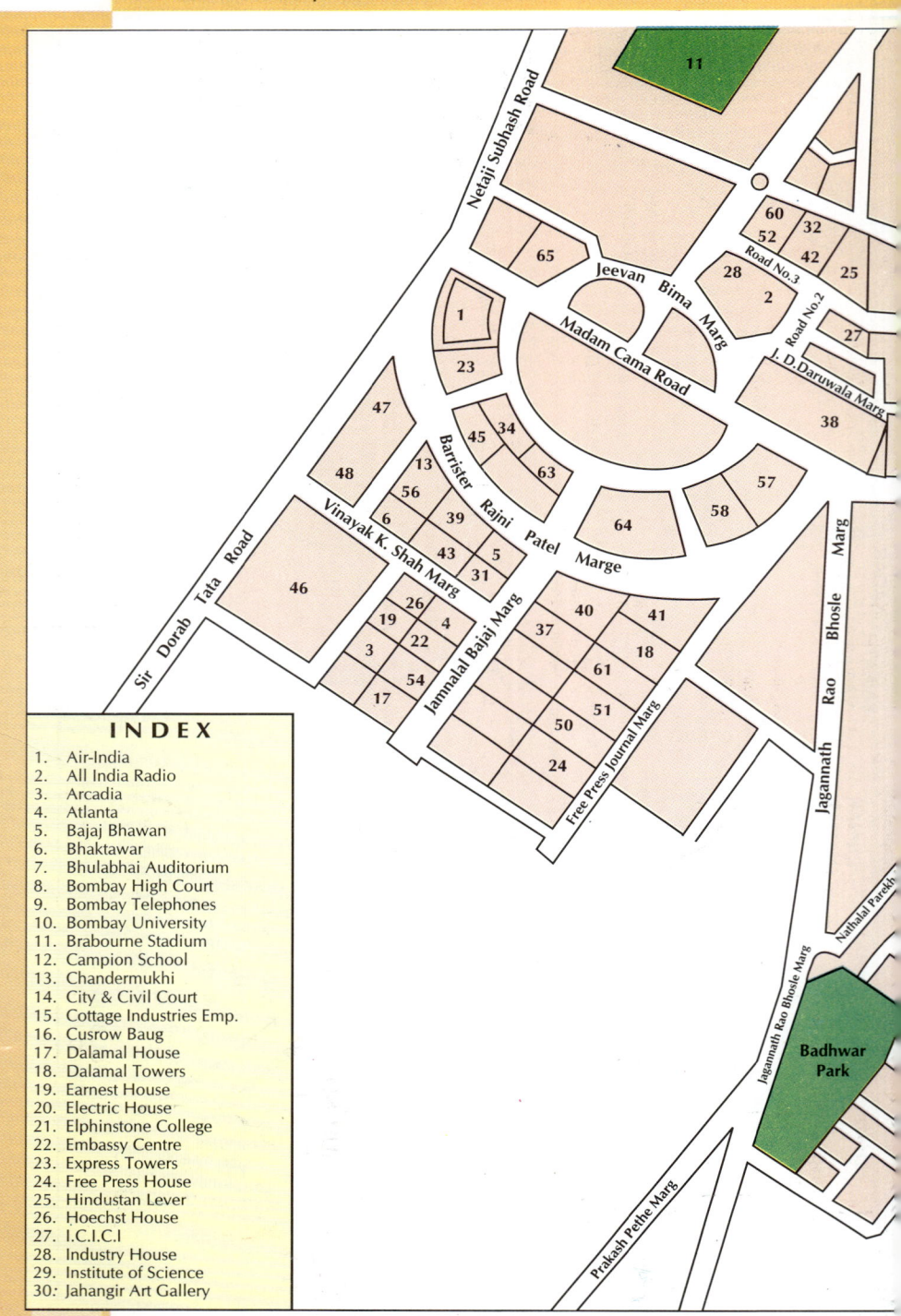

Nariman Point / Colaba

INDEX

1. Air-India
2. All India Radio
3. Arcadia
4. Atlanta
5. Bajaj Bhawan
6. Bhaktawar
7. Bhulabhai Auditorium
8. Bombay High Court
9. Bombay Telephones
10. Bombay University
11. Brabourne Stadium
12. Campion School
13. Chandermukhi
14. City & Civil Court
15. Cottage Industries Emp.
16. Cusrow Baug
17. Dalamal House
18. Dalamal Towers
19. Earnest House
20. Electric House
21. Elphinstone College
22. Embassy Centre
23. Express Towers
24. Free Press House
25. Hindustan Lever
26. Hoechst House
27. I.C.I.C.I
28. Industry House
29. Institute of Science
30. Jahangir Art Gallery

Nariman Point / Colaba

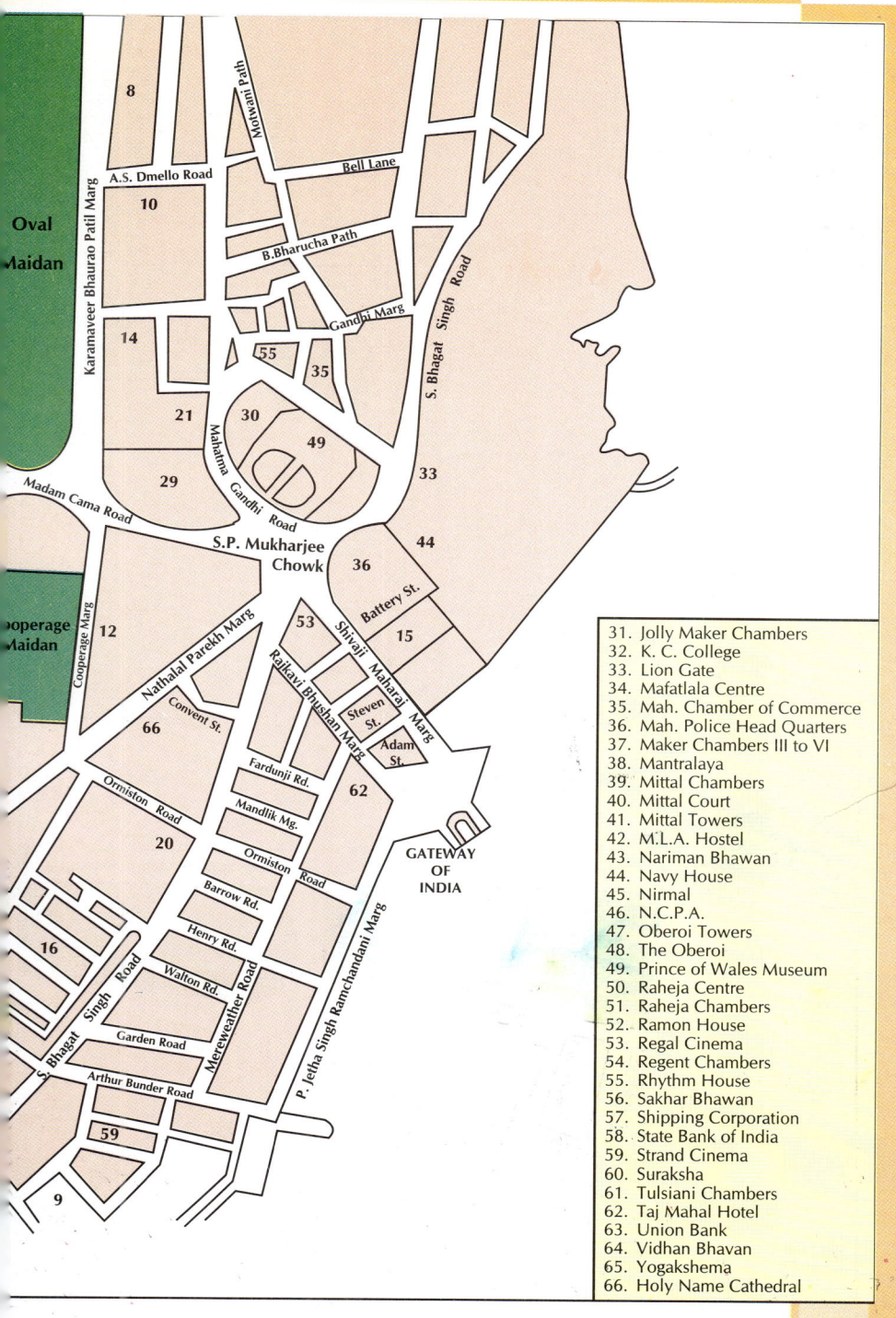

31. Jolly Maker Chambers
32. K. C. College
33. Lion Gate
34. Mafatlala Centre
35. Mah. Chamber of Commerce
36. Mah. Police Head Quarters
37. Maker Chambers III to VI
38. Mantralaya
39. Mittal Chambers
40. Mittal Court
41. Mittal Towers
42. M.L.A. Hostel
43. Nariman Bhawan
44. Navy House
45. Nirmal
46. N.C.P.A.
47. Oberoi Towers
48. The Oberoi
49. Prince of Wales Museum
50. Raheja Centre
51. Raheja Chambers
52. Ramon House
53. Regal Cinema
54. Regent Chambers
55. Rhythm House
56. Sakhar Bhawan
57. Shipping Corporation
58. State Bank of India
59. Strand Cinema
60. Suraksha
61. Tulsiani Chambers
62. Taj Mahal Hotel
63. Union Bank
64. Vidhan Bhavan
65. Yogakshema
66. Holy Name Cathedral

63

Horniman Circle

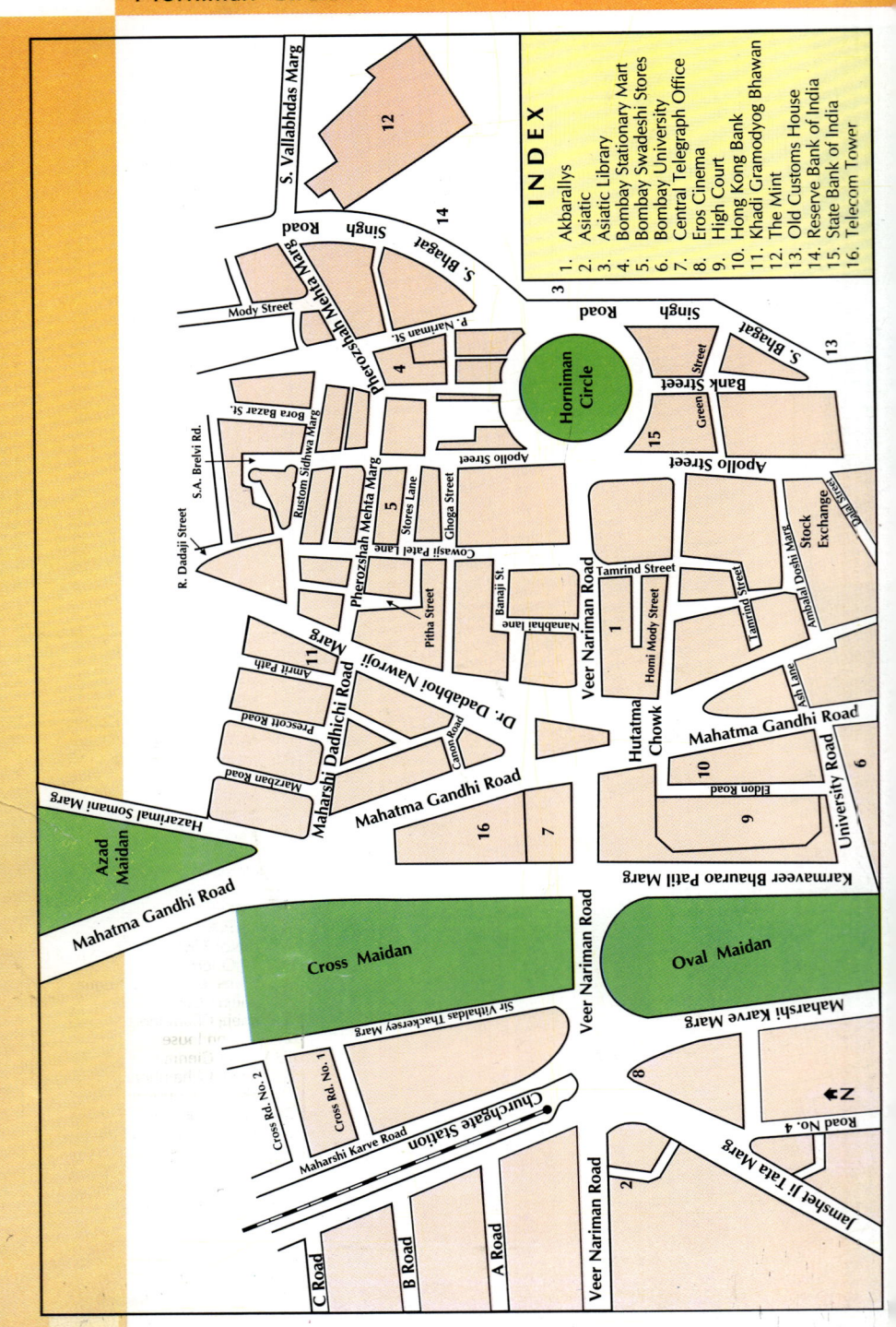

INDEX

1. Akbarallys
2. Asiatic
3. Asiatic Library
4. Bombay Stationary Mart
5. Bombay Swadeshi Stores
6. Bombay University
7. Central Telegraph Office
8. Eros Cinema
9. High Court
10. Hong Kong Bank
11. Khadi Gramodyog Bhawan
12. The Mint
13. Old Customs House
14. Reserve Bank of India
15. State Bank of India
16. Telecom Tower